Followers to Fortune

Building Your Social Media Empire

by
Pedro Barajas Jr

Table of Contents

Introduction

In an era where our daily lives are intertwined with social media, the prospect of going viral and transforming that visibility into a lucrative career or business is more feasible than ever before. This book is designed to be your road map through the intricate landscape of social media, guiding you through the process of growing your presence, mastering the algorithm, and ultimately, monetizing your platforms. Whether you're an aspiring influencer, a brand looking to expand its reach, or simply someone aiming to make a significant impact online, the journey starts here.

Understanding the algorithms that dictate what appears in our feeds is not just beneficial; it's essential for anyone looking to make a mark on social media. These invisible codes can be your greatest ally or your biggest obstacle. This book aims to demystify them for you, offering platform-specific tips alongside universal strategies that have been proven to encourage growth. By mastering these algorithms, you'll learn how to make them work for you, allowing your content to reach more eyes, engage more hearts, and attract more minds.

However, going viral is not just about understanding algorithms or crafting the perfect post. It's about connecting with your audience in a way that feels both genuine and impactful. It's about telling a story that resonates and compels others to share. Through a mix of practical advice, insider tips, and actionable strategies, this book will equip you with the tools you need to not only go viral but to also sustain that success and turn it into a profitable, fulfilling career. Ready? Let's dive in.

Chapter 1:
Laying the Foundation for
Your Social Media Empire

In today's digital age, creating a social media empire is more than a dream—it's a tangible reality for those willing to lay the groundwork and strategize effectively. The first step in this journey involves setting up your profiles to serve as the cornerstone of your digital presence. Carefully choosing the right platforms is crucial because each one has its unique audience and content style. Creating engaging bios and profiles isn't just about filling in the blanks; it's about crafting a narrative that resonates with your target audience. Speaking of which, understanding who you're trying to reach is vital. By defining your niche and analyzing your competitors, you'll gain insights into how to position yourself in the market. This chapter serves as the blueprint for building your social media empire. It's not just about getting followers; it's about laying the foundation for sustainable growth, engagement, and ultimately, monetization. Remember, every empire started with a single brick. In your case, it starts with understanding the basics and setting up your profiles for success.

Setting Up Your Profiles for Success

As we segue from understanding the foundational aspects of building your social media empire, it becomes crucial to focus on one of the initial steps to success: adequately setting up your profiles. It's about making a stellar first impression, yes, but it's also about the strategic, behind-the-scenes work that makes your profile not only visible but irresistibly engaging.

Think of your social media profile as your digital handshake. It's what people first encounter, and it sets the tone for the relationship you'll build with your audience. But how exactly do you ensure that this digital handshake is as powerful as possible? It starts with a sharp focus on choosing the right platforms for you, but it doesn't end there. From your bio to your visual identity, every element plays a crucial role in your success.

The process begins with a ruthless assessment of which social media platforms are most likely to connect you with your target audience. The allure of being everywhere at once can be strong, but spreading yourself too thin is a guaranteed recipe for diluted impact. Each platform has its quirks and its unique audience. Your strategy should be bespoke, crafted with precision to tap into the specific culture and characteristics of each platform you choose to dominate.

Your bio and profile are more than just a picture and a quick description; they are your elevator pitch to the world. Every word counts. Engaging bios are more than clever phrases; they tell a story, your story, in a way that resonates with your target audience. They convey not just what you do, but who you are and the unique value you bring to the table. A dash of personality, a hint of humor, and a clear call to action can transform a simple description into a powerful connector.

Visual consistency across your profiles strengthens your brand and makes you instantly recognizable across platforms. From your profile picture to your cover image and your posts, maintaining a consistent visual theme helps in cementing a solid and memorable brand identity. This doesn't mean every post must look the same, but they should all feel like unmistakably you.

Keywords play an underrated role in setting up your profile for success. Much like search engine optimization for websites, strategic use of relevant keywords in your social media profiles can vastly improve your visibility. Identify the keywords your target audience is using to search for content like yours, and then integrate them seamlessly into your bio, descriptions, and even your content.

A critical aspect often overlooked is the integration of cross-platform links in your profile. If you're active on multiple platforms, make sure your followers can find you across the social media landscape. This cross-pollination can help grow your audience faster by leveraging followers from one platform to build your presence on another.

Adapting your profile setup for mobile users is non-negotiable. With the majority of social media interactions happening on mobile devices, your profiles need to look just as good on a small screen as they do on a desktop. This means paying close attention to how images, bios, and even the arrangement of content appear on mobile devices.

The voice and tone of your profile should speak directly to your target audience. If you're aiming to inspire, motivate, or educate, your language and tone should reflect that. Consistency in your voice across posts and profiles helps in building a reliable and recognizable brand persona.

Privacy settings and account security are also paramount. While it's important to be accessible and engage with your audience, protecting your personal information and ensuring your accounts are secure from unauthorized access cannot be overlooked. Regularly updating passwords and reviewing privacy settings should be part of your social media routine.

Engagement prompts within your bio can be a clever tool to encourage interaction right off the bat. Questions, intriguing statements, or calls to action can inspire followers to engage with your content, comment on your posts, or share your profile with others. Engagement is currency in the social media world, and your profile should be designed to maximize it.

Schedule regular updates and reviews of your profile. The social media landscape is ever-evolving, and so should your profile be. Regularly refreshing your bio, profile images, and even reviewing your platform strategy ensures that your profile stays relevant and aligned with your current goals and audience expectations.

Don't forget to monitor the performance of your profile. Platforms often provide analytics that can offer insights into what's working and what isn't. Use this data to tweak your profile, adjust your strategy, and refine the content you share.

In summary, setting up your social media profiles for success is a blend of art and strategy. It requires a deep understanding of the platforms you choose, a clear articulation of your brand, and an ongoing commitment to adaptation and optimization. Your profile isn't just a static page on the internet; it's a dynamic, living representation of your brand and a crucial cornerstone of your social media empire.

Remember, the social media landscape is constantly shifting. What works today might not work tomorrow. Stay agile, keep learning, and keep refining your approach. Your efforts in setting up a magnetic, engaging, and strategically sound profile will pay dividends in the form of a growing, vibrant, and deeply engaged community.

Choosing the Right Platforms for You When setting your sights on becoming a social media sensation, it's tempting to jump on every platform available. However, spreading yourself too thin can be a recipe for burnout and inefficacy. Let's get granular and deliberate about selecting the social platforms that align best with your goals, content style, and target audience.

Think about your content's nature. Are you more into creating visually stunning images, or does your strength lie in charismatic video presentations? Platforms like Instagram and Pinterest are havens for those with an eye for photography and design, while YouTube and TikTok cater to those looking to engage through dynamic video content. It's all about playing to your strengths.

Your target demographic plays a significant role in this decision. Different platforms appeal to different age groups, geographic locations, and interests. If you're aiming to captivate the attention of Gen Z, TikTok and Snapchat are your go-to platforms. For a more millennial audience, Instagram and YouTube might be more your speed. It's crucial to hang out where your audience hangs out.

Don't forget to consider the type of engagement each platform is known for. Instagram is great for building a community that appreciates aesthetically pleasing content and stories. In contrast, Twitter's quick and direct communication style is perfect for sparking conversations and sharing opinions.

Another aspect to ponder over is the learning curve and the content creation tools required for each platform. Some platforms may necessitate a more profound knowledge of video editing, while others might be more straightforward, focusing solely on pictures or text. It's essential to assess whether you have the time and resources to master these skills or if you should start with platforms that align more closely with your current capabilities.

Understanding each platform's algorithm is also a key factor in your decision-making process. This insight can dramatically influence your content's visibility and engagement. Platforms like Facebook and Instagram have algorithms that prioritize content from family and friends over businesses and creators, making organic growth challenging. On the other hand, TikTok's algorithm seems to offer a more level playing field for content creators. We'll dive deeper into algorithms in Chapter 3, but for now, know that they should influence your platform choice.

Consider the potential for monetization on each platform. While your primary goal might be to share your passion or message, eventually, monetizing that audience can sustain and expand your efforts. Some platforms have clearer paths to monetization through ads, sponsored content, and affiliate marketing. Considering these options early on can help align your long-term goals with your platform selection.

Don't underestimate the value of experimentation. While it's wise to focus your efforts on one or two platforms initially, don't be afraid to test the waters on other platforms as you become more comfortable and your audience grows. Diversifying your social media presence can help ensure you're not putting all your eggs in one basket, especially as platforms evolve and audience preferences shift.

Networking with other content creators can also provide insights into which platforms are currently working well for them and why. These connections can offer invaluable firsthand experience that could influence your platform decisions. Remember, what works for one creator may not work for you, but understanding the reasons behind their choices can be enlightening.

In summary, choosing the right platforms is not about being everywhere at once. It's about strategically selecting the spaces where you can shine the brightest, connect most effectively with your intended audience, and ultimately, achieve your social media goals. As we delve into the nuances of profile creation in the next section, keep these platform considerations in mind to ensure your social media empire is built on the most fertile ground.

Creating Engaging Bios and Profiles is crucial for anyone looking to make a significant impact on social media. Your bio isn't just a set of words about you; it's your digital handshake, your elevator pitch, neatly condensed into a few impactful sentences. To grab attention and encourage follows, articulating your value proposition clearly and enticingly in this limited space is key. Think of your bio as your brand statement—a snapshot that tells users who you are, what you offer, and why they should care. Whether it's with a dash of humor, a professional tone, or a creative flair, ensure your bio resonates with your target audience while staying true to your personal or brand identity.

First things first, clarity is king. Your bio should communicate the essence of your brand or personal identity quickly. Users scroll through countless profiles daily, so you have a fleeting moment to make an impression. Use straightforward, accessible language and avoid industry jargon that might alienate potential followers. If you can, weave in keywords related to your niche without overstuffing. This not only helps users instantly recognize if your content aligns with their interests but also aids in discoverability within the platform's search function.

Equally important is injecting personality into your bio. Social media thrives on authenticity and connection. Sharing a quirky fact, a motto you live by, or even incorporating emojis relevant to your brand can make your profile more relatable and memorable. If you're stumped, think about how friends would describe you or the unique perspectives you bring to your field. These personal touches can turn a generic bio into a compelling reason to follow you.

Don't forget about the strategic use of links in your bio. Most platforms allow for at least a single website link, so make it count. Whether it's a link to your latest content, a landing page for newsletter sign-ups, or your portfolio, this is a crucial step for converting followers into subscribers or customers. Some platforms offer the option to include multiple links, or you can use link-in-bio tools to create a mobile landing page that houses everything you want your followers to find. Use this feature wisely to guide your audience towards meaningful engagement beyond the social media platform.

Lastly, updating your bio regularly can keep your profile fresh and reflect any shifts in your focus or achievements. A new certification, product launch, or even updating your current favorite quote can reinvigorate interest in your profile. Think of your bio as a living document, an aspect of your social media presence that evolves with you. When done right, creating an engaging bio and profile isn't just about standing out—it's about laying the foundation for lasting connections and driving engagement on your terms.

Understanding Your Target Audience

Now that you've got your profiles set up and shining, it's time to dive deep into one of the key factors that will dictate your success in the digital realm: understanding your target audience. This isn't just about knowing who they are but truly understanding what drives them, what their pains are, and what joy looks like to them in the context of the content you're creating. It's about empathy and connection on a level that transcends mere demographics.

First off, get clear on who it is you're trying to reach. This goes beyond age, location, and gender. What are their interests? What challenges are they facing? And importantly, how can you and your content be the solution they didn't even know they were searching for? This is where defining your niche and analyzing your competitors, as we'll explore in the following sections, plays a crucial role. By identifying the unique intersection of your passions and the needs of your audience, you set the stage for impactful, engaging content.

Understand that your audience isn't a static entity. They evolve, and so should your understanding of them. This means keeping a finger on the pulse of not just what they're saying explicitly but tapping into broader cultural, economic, and social trends that influence their worldview and preferences. Social listening tools can be invaluable here, providing insights into the conversation themes and sentiment around your niche.

Engaging directly with your audience is another non-negotiable. Beyond just responding to comments and messages, seek to understand their perspective, ask for their opinions, and encourage them to share their stories. These interactions not only deepen your understanding but also build a community vibe around your brand that's magnetic.

Another critical aspect is leveraging analytics. Most social platforms offer rich data on who's interacting with your content and how. Dive into this regularly, not just to see what's working but to understand who is responding. This information can help refine not just your content but your entire strategic approach.

Visualization can also be a powerful tool in audience understanding. Creating personas based on your research and interactions can help make the abstract idea of a "target audience" more concrete and relatable. Think of these personas as composite sketches of segments within your audience, each with their preferences, pain points, and what they find entertaining or valuable.

Remember, the goal here is not to appeal to everyone. In the quest for viral content and a massive follower count, it's easy to think that broader is better. However, the magic lies in specificity. When you speak directly to your core audience's hearts and minds, your content resonates more deeply, driving engagement and sharing that extends your reach far more effectively than a scattergun approach ever could.

Lastly, keep training your empathetic muscles. Understanding your audience is about getting into their shoes and viewing the world from their eyes. The more adept you become at this, the more intuitively you'll be able to generate content ideas, predict trends, and navigate shifts in the digital landscape that impact your audience.

In summary, understanding your target audience is a dynamic and ongoing process that forms the bedrock of your social media strategy. It's about much more than demographics. It's about connection, empathy, and the continuous interplay between speaking and listening. As you get to know your audience better, you'll find your content not just seen but felt, and that's when you know you're on the right track.

Armed with a deep understanding of your audience, you're now well-equipped to take the next steps in crafting a content strategy that not only captures attention but also hearts. So, let's delve into the art and science of content creation, where you'll learn to balance quality and quantity, discover engaging content ideas for any niche, and leverage the undeniable power of visuals. The foundation is laid; now let's start building your empire.

Defining Your Niche As we pivot from understanding the broad strokes of setting up your social media profiles to diving deeper into the heart of your strategy, a pivotal step awaits—defining your niche. The essence of your online persona and the core of your content strategy hinge upon this crucial element. It's about carving out a segment of the vast digital landscape where you can shine the brightest, making your mark by catering to specific needs, interests, or curiosities that resonate with a specific audience.

Imagine social media as an immense ocean, teeming with fish of every imaginable type. Now, if you're trying to catch something, would you rather cast a wide net and hope for the best, or would you use a specific type of bait known to attract the fish you're actually interested in? Defining your niche is akin to selecting the right bait. It ensures that your efforts are targeted, your message is clear, and you're not wasting resources trying to appeal to everyone under the sun.

A common pitfall for many aspiring social media titans is attempting to be everything to everyone. While versatility is an admirable trait, social media thrives on specificity. Think about the YouTube channels, Instagram profiles, or Twitter personalities that have truly made a mark—chances are, they started with a very focused idea or theme. Whether it's fashion, travel, gaming, wellness, or any other sector, they stood out because they dove deep into their chosen field, carving out a niche that allowed them to become viewed as authorities or go-to sources in that space.

How does one go about identifying their niche? It starts with self-reflection. Assess your passions, hobbies, and areas of expertise. What do you love talking about? What could you produce content about tirelessly without running out of steam? It's essential to choose a niche that not only has an audience but is also something you're genuinely excited about. Authenticity resonates with audiences, and if you're passionate about your content, it will shine through, attracting like-minded individuals.

Next, consider the market demand. Is there an audience for the niche you're interested in? Utilizing tools like keyword research and social media analytics can provide insights into what people are searching for and talking about. If there seems to be a gap in the market that aligns with your interests, you might have found your perfect niche. However, if it's an area with high demand but also high competition, think about how you can narrow it down further or approach it from a unique angle that sets you apart.

Understanding your audience is another integral aspect of defining your niche. Who are they? What do they care about? Engaging with potential audience members through social media polls, surveys, or browsing through relevant forums and comment sections can give you valuable insights into their preferences and pain points. This understanding enables you to tailor your content more effectively, striking a chord with the very people you aim to attract.

Competition isn't something to shy away from; it's an opportunity for learning. Analyzing your competitors can offer clues about what works and what doesn't within your chosen niche. Notice the types of content that receive the most engagement, the way they communicate with their audience, and even what they could be doing better. Then, use this information to refine your own strategy, ensuring you deliver value in a way that is uniquely yours.

Let's also talk about flexibility. While defining your niche, it's crucial to strike a balance between being specific and being so narrow that you corner yourself. As you grow and as trends shift, you might find that your niche evolves. That's perfectly normal and healthy. The key is to remain relevant and true to what your audience needs and wants from you, even if that means making adjustments along the way.

Finally, documenting your niche and content strategy can provide clarity and direction. It allows you to articulate your mission, understand your audience, and plan your content with purpose. Keep this document dynamic, revisiting and revising it as your social media empire expands and your understanding of your audience deepens.

In conclusion, defining your niche isn't just about finding a small corner of the internet where you can fit in. It's about creating a space where you can thrive, innovate, and lead. It's the foundation upon which your content, engagement, and ultimately, your social media success is built. Take the time to do it right, and you'll find that this focus not only makes your journey more enjoyable but also more fruitful in the long run.

Analyzing Your Competitors Diving into the world of social media without a solid understanding of your competition is like setting sail without a compass. It's crucial, then, to take a deep dive into analyzing your competitors as this can provide invaluable insights into what works, what doesn't, and where there might be gaps that you can exploit. This knowledge not only prevents you from repeating the mistakes of others but also helps in tailoring your strategies to stand out.

Begin with identifying who your main competitors are. These are profiles or brands within your niche that target a similar audience or offer comparable products or services. Use social media tools and simple manual search techniques to list them. Once you have your list, start by observing their content strategy – what kind of posts are receiving high engagement rates? What times are they posting? Analysis of these patterns can offer clues into effective practices in your niche.

Next, engage with their community. This doesn't mean intruding but rather observing the types of conversations happening around their posts. What is their audience praising or criticizing? Understanding audience sentiment towards your competitors can provide strategic insights into how you can differentiate your brand and content. Perhaps there's a consistent complaint that you can solve or an unaddressed desire you can fulfill.

Also, note how your competitors utilize different social media platforms. Some might be heavily investing in Instagram stories and reels, while others see more engagement on Facebook live sessions. This visibility into platform-specific strategies can help you decide where to focus your efforts or diversify your content to capture a wider audience.

Lastly, don't forget to observe any growth hacks or promotional strategies they are using, such as partnerships with influencers, contests, or hashtags. These tactics can be quite telling of what drives user engagement and growth within your niche. However, it's crucial to adapt, not copy. Your goal is to learn from the competition and then innovate to provide unique value to your audience. Harnessing these insights, you're well on your way to developing a competitive strategy that's not only responsive but proactive in the dynamic world of social media.

Chapter 2:
Content is King

In the vast kingdom of social media, content wears the crown and wields the scepter. It's not just any content, though; what you need is material that captivates, engages, and resonates deeply with your audience. You've already laid the groundwork by setting up your profiles and understanding your audience, but now it's time to craft a strategy that consistently delivers content so compelling it can't help but attract followers. This chapter unpacks the essence of creating content that not only stands out but also aligns seamlessly with your goals of growing, monetizing, and going viral on your chosen platforms. Think of your content as your voice in the digital realm—a voice that should be authentic, consistent, and tailored to speak volumes to those listening. Here, we dive into crafting a content strategy that balances quality with quantity, ensuring you're equipped to produce engaging material that speaks directly to your niche. We'll explore the undeniable power of visuals, from photos that tell a story at a glance to videos that keep viewers hooked till the very end, and provide you with the tools to create eye-catching content that captures hearts and minds. Remember, in the ever-evolving landscape of social media, content isn't just king—it's the key to unlocking unimaginable growth and success.

Crafting Your Content Strategy

As we transition from understanding the bedrock of your social media presence, it's time to dive into the lifeblood of your online identity -

your content. Without an effective content strategy, even the most robust foundation will struggle to attract and retain an audience. Your content isn't just about what you post but how, why, and when you post it.

Firstly, identifying your core message is crucial. This becomes the centerpiece around which all your content orbits. Ask yourself, what is the primary takeaway you want your audience to have? This clarity will act as your north star, guiding your content creation process.

Understanding your audience cannot be overstressed. Your content strategy should be crafted with your audience's preferences, pain points, and pleasures in mind. Dive deep into analytics, conduct surveys, and engage in direct conversations to glean insights about your audience. This knowledge allows for the creation of content that resonates and engages effectively.

Consistency in branding and voice plays a significant role in making your content memorable. Your audience should be able to recognize your content across platforms without blatant signage. This familiarity builds trust and strengthens your community.

Diversification of content types is essential in keeping your audience engaged. In the digital realm, monotony is your enemy. Mix up your content with videos, infographics, blogs, and live sessions to cater to different audience preferences and keep your feed fresh.

Speaking of keeping things fresh, timing and frequency matter significantly. Finding the sweet spot for when and how often to post can dramatically affect your content's performance. Use platform analytics to make data-driven decisions on optimal posting times and frequencies.

Engagement should always be a two-way street. Crafting content that encourages interaction not only boosts your visibility thanks to algorithms but also builds a stronger relationship between you and your audience. Open-ended questions, calls to action, and topical discussions can serve as great engagement tools.

Quality, while balancing with quantity, cannot be compromised. In a world saturated with content, yours needs to stand out. Invest time in creating well-researched, beautifully presented, and genuinely engaging content. Remember, subpar content published just to maintain frequency can hurt your brand more than it helps.

Leverage user-generated content whenever possible. Not only does it provide you with a repository of content to share, but it also increases community involvement and commitment. When your audience sees their content being celebrated, it encourages further participation and loyalty.

Storytelling should be at the heart of your strategy. The most impactful content often tells a story that the audience can connect with on an emotional level. Whether it's the story behind your brand, the journey of a customer, or a cause your community cares about, narratives have the power to engage deeply.

Always be prepared to adapt. The digital landscape shifts rapidly, and flexibility in your content strategy is vital. Keep abreast of trends, platform updates, and shifts in your audience's behavior to tweak your strategy as needed efficiently.

Data should dictate decisions. Your strategy should be a mix of creativity and analytics. Regularly review your content's performance across different metrics to understand what works and what doesn't. let data insights guide your future content creation and strategy adjustments.

Never lose sight of your objectives. Whether it's brand awareness, lead generation, sales, or community building, every piece of content should serve a purpose. Having clear goals for different content pieces helps in measuring success and ROI.

Innovate and experiment. The digital space rewards bravery. Don't be afraid to try new formats, platforms, or messaging. Monitor results closely and learn from every experiment to continually refine your strategy.

Finally, remember the importance of patience and persistence. Rome wasn't built in a day, and neither will your social media empire be. Stick to your strategy, make informed adjustments, and over time, you'll see your efforts come to fruition. Crafting a winning content strategy is a journey, not a quick sprint. Embrace the process, and you'll be rewarded with a loyal, engaged, and growing audience.

Balancing Quality and Quantity In the fast-paced world of social media, one of the most challenging dilemmas creators face is finding the perfect balance between quality and quantity. It's a tightrope walk that can significantly impact your ability to grow, monetize, and even go viral on these platforms. Let's dive into strategies that harmonize this balance, enabling you to master the algorithm while consistently engaging your audience.

First and foremost, understanding that not every post needs to be a magnum opus is crucial. While it's essential to maintain a standard of quality that reflects well on your brand, spinning your wheels on perfection for every post can hinder your ability to post consistently. The algorithms favor regular engagement, so finding a middle ground where you can produce content that is both high-quality and frequent is your golden ticket. This often means planning content in batches and making judicious use of scheduling tools to ensure a steady stream of posts.

Yet, quality should never be sacrificed on the altar of quantity. Each piece of content should serve a purpose, whether to inform, entertain, or engage. This is where the analytics come into play. Regularly reviewing which types of posts perform best allows you to tweak your strategy, focusing on what works best. By integrating feedback loops into your content creation process, you're able to maintain a quality that resonates with your audience while fine-tuning the frequency of your posts for optimal engagement.

Another dynamic aspect of balancing quality and quantity is the trend factor. Social media trends can skyrocket your visibility when leveraged correctly. Jumping on these trends requires a swift content creation process that doesn't always allow for the same level of polish as your regular posts. However, participating in trends can expose your brand to a broader audience, increasing your chances of going viral. It's a strategic play that, when balanced with your evergreen, high-quality content, can significantly amplify your reach.

Lastly, don't underestimate the power of user-generated content and collaborations. These can be goldmines for increasing the volume of your content without sacrificing quality. Encouraging your community to share their own stories and content related to your brand not only fosters a stronger connection with your audience but also provides you with additional quality content to share. Collaborations with other creators can fill your content calendar, bringing fresh perspectives and value to your audience while allowing you a bit more breathing room to focus on high-quality cornerstone content pieces.

In conclusion, the dance between quality and quantity on social media is delicate but manageable. By being strategic about content planning, leveraging analytics, jumping on trends, and incorporating user-generated content and collaborations, you can maintain a balance that propels your growth. Remember, it's about making every piece of content count, engaging regularly with your audience, and always being ready to adapt to the ever-evolving landscape of social media.

Engaging Content Ideas for Any Niche Whether you're a seasoned social media strategist or just starting to carve out your digital empire, one truth remains constant: content reigns supreme. Yet, the relentless quest for the next engaging post can seem daunting, especially when you're trying to stand out in an oversaturated market. Let's break down this barrier by diving into a treasure trove of content ideas that can spark engagement, foster community, and set any niche alight with excitement.

First off, storytelling has a universal appeal. Even the most seemingly mundane product or service can transform into something captivating with the right narrative. Think about crafting content that shares the journey of your brand, the stories behind your products, or even customer success stories. This approach not only humanizes your brand but also builds a deeper connection with your audience. Everyone loves a compelling story, and every niche has its own tales waiting to be told.

Next, consider how-to guides and tutorials. These can be absolute gold in any niche, offering real value to your audience and positioning your brand as a go-to resource. Whether it's a step-by-step guide, a video tutorial, or an infographic, educational content can help solve problems and answer questions. This type of content not only engages but also encourages shares, as people are more likely to share something that they find practical and helpful.

Don't underestimate the power of user-generated content (UGC). Encouraging your audience to share their own stories, photos, or videos using your product or service can lead to a wealth of authentic and relatable content. UGC not only reduces your content creation workload but also amplifies trust in your brand. It's a testament to the real-world impact of your offerings and can resonate well across different demographics within your niche.

Finally, tapping into trends and challenges can offer a timely and engaging twist to your content strategy. While it's essential to stay true to your brand voice, aligning with current events or viral challenges can increase your brand's visibility and engagement. However, it's important to approach trends with a strategic mindset, ensuring they align with your brand values and resonate with your target audience. Done right, trend-based content can provide a significant boost to your social media presence, propelling your message far and wide across the digital landscape.

In conclusion, creating engaging content doesn't have to be a struggle, regardless of your niche. By weaving storytelling into your strategy, offering valuable how-to guides, embracing user-generated content, and strategically participating in trends, you can build a content library that not only captivates but converts. Remember, the key to success in the digital realm is not just to attract attention but to build connections and provide value, turning your audience into a community.

The Power of Visuals

In the realm of social media, visuals are not merely an element of content strategy; they wield unparalleled power to captivate, engage, and persuade audiences. As we delve into the significance of visuals within the overarching theme of "Content is King," it becomes clear that understanding and utilizing imagery is pivotal for anyone aiming to make an impact on social media platforms.

Visuals command immediate attention, unlike text which demands time to digest. This instant appeal is why platforms teeming with photos, videos, and infographics often see higher levels of user engagement. Think of it this way: when scrolling through a feed, it's the striking image or the dynamic video thumbnail that halts the scroll, not necessarily a well-written headline. The brain processes visuals at lightning speed, turning images into language and emotions that resonate on a personal level with viewers.

Incorporating visuals into your content isn't just about beautification; it's about communication. A well-crafted image or video can convey complex messages succinctly, breaking down barriers of misunderstanding and forging a quicker connection with your audience. This is invaluable in a world where attention spans are fleeting, and the battle for eyes on your content is fierce.

However, leveraging the power of visuals isn't just about quantity; it's profoundly about quality. High-quality, relevant visuals not only enhance aesthetic appeal but also bolster your brand's credibility. They signal that you value your audience's attention and are committed to providing content that is both visually appetizing and meaningful. Moreover, consistency in visual styling across your posts can reinforce brand recognition, making your content easily identifiable amid the noise.

Let's not overlook the storytelling potential of visuals. Stories evoke emotions, and emotions catalyze engagement and sharing. Through images and videos, you can craft narratives that speak volumes, touching hearts and sparking conversations. This storytelling can significantly amplify the virality of your content, as viewers are more likely to share content that moved them emotionally.

The advent of various tools has democratized access to creating eye-catching content. From user-friendly photo-editing apps to comprehensive design platforms, the resources at your disposal are vast and versatile. These tools not only help in refining images but also empower users with no professional design experience to produce professional-grade visuals. Investing time in mastering these resources can dramatically uplift your visual content game.

Engagement metrics on visual content often exceed those of text-only posts. Likes, shares, comments, and even saves paint a telling picture: visuals resonate and engage. By analyzing these metrics, one can fine-tune their visual strategy, identifying what types of imagery spark the most interaction and tailoring content accordingly.

In the context of going viral, visuals are your best bet. They are shareable, memorable, and capable of crossing linguistic and cultural barriers. A compelling image or an engaging video can traverse communities, countries, and continents, garnering views and interactions that text posts often cannot achieve.

For those looking to grow, monetize, and perhaps most importantly, master the algorithm, an emphasis on visuals is non-negotiable. Algorithms favor content that engages, and nothing engages quite like powerful imagery. As you harness the visual aspect of your content strategy, you're not just creating posts; you're optimizing for visibility, engagement, and ultimately, the viral potential.

Remember, in the digital kingdom where content reigns supreme, visuals are the crown jewels. They enhance the appeal, extend the reach, and amplify the impact of your content. In leveraging the power of visuals, you unlock new dimensions of storytelling, engagement, and growth on social media platforms. It's not just about seeing; it's about being seen and remembered. Thus, in your quest to dominate social media, let visuals be your ally, and wield them with strategy and creativity.

Leveraging Photos and Videos In the ever-evolving landscape of social media, the power of visual content cannot be overstated. Photos and videos stand out as compelling tools that can significantly amplify your online presence, attract a broader audience, and enhance engagement on your platforms. The visual appeal is not just about aesthetics; it's about creating a visceral connection with your audience, conveying your message more effectively, and ultimately, driving more interactions which are crucial for mastering the algorithm and achieving virality.

First and foremost, it's essential to understand the type of visuals that resonate most with your target audience. This insight is critical because what works for a fashion influencer may not hold the same appeal for a tech vlogger. Experiment with different types of content - behind-the-scenes shots, product teasers, user-generated content, and instructional videos, just to name a few. Pay attention to the feedback and engagement each type receives, as this data is invaluable for refining your strategy and ensuring your content aligns with your audience's preferences.

Moreover, the quality of your photos and videos plays a significant role in how they're perceived by both your followers and the algorithms of social media platforms. High-quality, well-edited visuals are more likely to be shared, liked, and commented on, increasing your visibility and helping you to grow your platform. Investing in a good camera or hiring a professional photographer can make a difference, but even smartphones nowadays are equipped with powerful cameras that, when used correctly, can produce stunning content. Learning basic photo and video editing techniques can also elevate your content, making it stand out in a sea of mediocrity.

Storytelling through visuals is another aspect that shouldn't be underestimated. Photos and videos that tell a story, evoke emotions, or share a unique perspective tend to perform better. They're not only more engaging but also more shareable, which can exponentially increase your reach. Think about how you can use visuals to narrate your brand's story, show the human side behind your business, or share relatable experiences. Authenticity in these stories can foster a deeper connection with your audience, making them more loyal and engaged.

Last but not least, consistency in visual branding across your social media platforms can significantly impact your brand's perception and recognition. Utilizing a consistent color scheme, style, and format helps in creating a cohesive look that is instantly recognizable to your followers. This doesn't mean every photo or video should look the same, but there should be a coherent visual theme running through your content. Strategic use of visuals, when aligned with your overall social media strategy, can indeed be a game-changer in growing your presence, making fortune, and mastering the intricacies of social media algorithms.

Tools for Creating Eye-Catching Content Diving into the digital world, where the competition for eyes and clicks never sleeps, necessitates a toolkit that's both dynamic and capable of producing content that stands out. To really make an impression, you need more than just a keen eye for trends; you need the tools that can turn your ideas into visually stunning realities. Here, we're mapping out a treasure chest of such tools, designed to elevate your content from good to unmissable.

First off, let's talk about graphic design software. Platforms like Adobe Creative Cloud, which includes Photoshop and Illustrator, offer extensive features for those looking to create professional-grade graphics. However, the learning curve can be steep. For a more user-friendly experience that still delivers high-quality results, tools like Canva or PicMonkey provide intuitive design interfaces, templates, and resources perfect for crafting social media posts, banners, and other visuals without needing a degree in graphic design. The key here is to choose a tool that matches your skill level and design needs, making the creation process as efficient as possible.

When it comes to video content, the stakes are even higher. Video editing software like Adobe Premiere Pro or Final Cut Pro offers a robust set of features for those looking to dive deep into video creation. But for those who want to keep it simple yet effective, apps like InShot or Quik by GoPro offer easy-to-use interfaces for editing videos right from your phone. Incorporating text overlays, music, and transitions can transform basic footage into engaging content that grabs and holds attention.

Don't forget the importance of high-quality images. In an era where smartphones can produce stunning high-resolution photos, apps like Lightroom Mobile and VSCO are indispensable for photo editing on the go. Adjusting lighting, applying presets, or tweaking colors can enhance the visual appeal of your images, making them more likely to catch the viewer's eye and generate engagement.

Lastly, it's crucial to stay organized and efficient. Tools like Trello or Asana for project management, and Buffer or Hootsuite for scheduling and publishing, can streamline your content creation workflow. They allow you to plan ahead, collaborate with team members, and ensure your content is consistent and timely. Implementing these tools into your strategy can save you time and stress, letting you focus on the creative aspects of content creation that truly move the needle.

Chapter 3:
Mastering the Algorithm

Transitioning from crafting your content strategy, it's time to confront the behemoth that decides who sees your painstakingly created content: the algorithm. Understanding the foundational mechanics of social media algorithms is akin to unlocking a treasure chest in the digital age. It's not about tricking the system but harmonizing your content with the underlying rhythms of platforms like Facebook, Instagram, and YouTube. Each platform dances to its own beat, and in this chapter, we'll dissect these nuances, offering you a map to navigate through their complexities.

Algorithms can seem like inscrutable gatekeepers, but they follow logical patterns, primarily focusing on engagement and relevance to determine content distribution. Recognizing this, adjusting your content strategy based on the analytical feedback you receive is not just beneficial; it's essential. Analyzing performance metrics allows for a deeper understanding of what resonates with your audience and how you can fine-tune your postings for maximum visibility and engagement.

While it might feel like you're at the mercy of these algorithms, remember, they are, at their core, designed to prioritize user experience. By aligning your content creation with strategies that enhance this experience, you aren't just playing into the hands of the algorithm; you're also elevating the quality of your engagement with your community. This chapter will guide you through understanding these complex systems, ensuring your content doesn't just reach your audience but also captivates them.

The Basics of Social Media Algorithms

Understanding the nuts and bolts of social media algorithms is your first step towards mastering them. At its core, an algorithm is a set of rules or a formula that social media platforms use to determine what content gets shown to users, when it's shown, and to whom. It's like a filter that sifts through the vast amount of information and picks out what it thinks a user will find most engaging or relevant.

One fundamental thing to grasp is that these algorithms are designed with the user's experience in mind. Platforms like Instagram, Facebook, and Twitter prioritize content they believe will keep users on the platform longer. This means the algorithm favors content that is engaging, interactive, and likely to spur conversation.

How does this affect you? Well, when you understand what types of content are favored by the platform's algorithms, you can tailor your content strategy to increase the likelihood of your posts appearing in your audience's feeds. This involves creating content that sparks interest and interaction, such as posts that encourage comments, shares, and likes.

Moreover, it's crucial to recognize that these algorithms aren't static; they're constantly evolving. Social media platforms frequently tweak their algorithms to improve user experience and adapt to new trends. This means what worked yesterday might not work tomorrow, necessitating vigilance and adaptability in your strategy.

Timeliness is another important factor. Most social media platforms have an element of recency in their algorithms, favoring content that is recent and therefore more likely to be relevant. This underscores the importance of posting regularly and at times when your audience is most active on the platform.

Engagement is the currency of the social media realm. The more engagement your posts generate, the more favorable the algorithms will view them. This doesn't mean you should aim for likes and comments at the expense of quality, but it does mean you should be strategic in crafting content that invites interaction.

Another aspect to consider is the role of personalization in these algorithms. Platforms like Facebook use signals such as past interactions, friend lists, and user interests to tailor the content in a user's feed. This personalized content curation means that understanding your audience and what they like is more important than ever.

Now, how do you leverage this knowledge? Start by analyzing your most successful posts. Look for patterns in what resonates with your audience. Is it a particular topic, a type of visual, or maybe a format like polls or quizzes? Once you identify what works, aim to replicate and innovate on that success.

Consistency is key, not just in the quality of your content, but in your engagement with the platform. Algorithms often favor users who are active and regularly contribute to the community. This means posting consistently, yes, but also interacting with your followers, replying to comments, and engaging with other users' content.

Remember, the ultimate aim of social media platforms is to keep users engaged and on their site for as long as possible. If your content aligns with this goal, by being genuinely interesting, entertaining, or informative, you're more likely to be favored by the algorithm.

Also, don't forget about the power of experimentation. The only way to truly know what works is to try different strategies and analyze the results. Social media platforms often provide analytics tools that allow you to track the performance of your posts and understand your audience better.

When it comes to mastering social media algorithms, there's no one-size-fits-all solution. Each platform has its own set of rules and priorities. While the principles of engaging, quality content are universal, the specifics can vary significantly from one platform to the next.

In the following sections, we'll delve deeper into platform-specific strategies for Facebook, Instagram, YouTube, and more. But regardless of the platform, remember that understanding and adapting to the algorithm is a continuous process. It requires a blend of creativity, analysis, and, most importantly, a genuine desire to connect with and provide value to your audience.

The basics of social media algorithms aren't just technical rules to follow; they're a reminder of the importance of creating meaningful, engaging content. By focusing on your audience's needs and leveraging the algorithms to your advantage, you can maximize your visibility, grow your following, and achieve your social media goals.

So, take what you've learned here as your foundation and get ready to dive deeper into the intricacies of each platform. With patience, persistence, and a data-driven approach, you'll be well on your way to mastering the social media algorithm and unlocking the full potential of your online presence.

Platform-Specific Tips

Navigating social media platforms can sometimes feel like decoding a complex puzzle. Each platform has its quirks, tricks, and secret handshakes that can either catapult your content to viral status or let it languish in obscurity. Understanding these nuances is not just beneficial; it's critical. Here, we're diving deep into the tips that can help you master the algorithm on several key platforms.

Starting with **Facebook**, remember that engagement rules the roost. It's not just about the number of likes; it's the comments, shares, and even the types of reactions your posts receive that matter. A well-timed poll or an engaging video can work wonders. Videos, especially, tend to have higher engagement rates, so incorporate them into your strategy. Also, leveraging Facebook Groups can amplify your reach significantly. These are communities waiting to hear from you, so don't overlook them.

When it comes to **Instagram**, aesthetics are key. This platform is all about the visuals, so high-quality photos and videos are non-negotiable. However, don't forget about the power of stories and Reels. These features offer fantastic ways to connect with your audience more casually and personally. Moreover, Instagram's algorithm favors content that generates conversations, so crafting captions that encourage comments is a smart move. Lastly, don't underestimate the power of timely posts; understanding when your audience is most active can significantly boost your visibility.

Moving to **YouTube**, it's a universe of content where consistency and quality reign supreme. Here, understanding your niche and providing value is critical. Whether it's through tutorials, entertainments, or informational videos, make sure your content stands out. Also, remember that YouTube is the second largest search engine, so SEO is a big deal here. Using the right keywords in your titles, descriptions, and tags can make a huge difference in how easily people can find your videos.

Now, while these tips are specific to these platforms, there are some general strategies that hold true across the board. For instance, understanding the best times to post can help your content gain initial traction. Similarly, keeping a close eye on your analytics can offer insights into what works and what doesn't, allowing you to tweak your strategy for better results.

Another universal tip is the importance of interaction. Engaging with your audience by responding to comments, asking questions, and even engaging with other creators' content can help boost your algorithmic appeal. Social media platforms favor content that fosters community and interaction, so make this a priority.

Hashtags are another tool that, while their importance varies from platform to platform, can significantly increase your content's discoverability. On Instagram, for example, well-researched hashtags can expose your posts to a broader audience. Meanwhile, on YouTube, hashtags are less visible but can still help categorize your content for more targeted discovery.

Live streaming is another powerful feature across multiple platforms, offering real-time engagement that can do wonders for your algorithmic footprint. Whether it's an AMA (Ask Me Anything) on Instagram, a live Q&A on Facebook, or a live tutorial on YouTube, these sessions can drive significant engagement and audience growth.

User-generated content is a goldmine that's often underutilized. Encouraging your followers to create content related to your brand or niche not only boosts engagement but also provides you with a wealth of content to share, further nurturing your community.

Cross-promotion is another strategy that, while simple, is extremely effective. Leveraging your presence on one platform to grow another can be as simple as sharing your Instagram Reels on Facebook or linking your YouTube video in your Instagram bio. This multi-platform presence ensures you're reaching your audience wherever they are.

Lastly, staying updated with the platforms' constant updates and changes is crucial. What worked a year ago might not work today, and new features are always around the corner. Staying flexible and willing to adapt your strategies accordingly is key to long-term success.

In conclusion, mastering social media platforms doesn't have to be a shot in the dark. By understanding the unique characteristics and algorithms of each platform, you can tailor your strategy to maximize your reach and engagement. Remember, success on social media is part continuous learning, part persistence, and wholly about creating value for your audience. Keep these platform-specific tips in mind, and you'll be well on your way to growing your social media empire.

Facebook carries a reputation for being the elder statesman in the family of social media platforms, yet it remains a potent channel for viral growth and monetization when navigated with expertise. The key to mastering Facebook's algorithm lies in understanding its unique blend of content preferences, engagement metrics, and user behavior, molding your strategy to leverage these elements effectively.

First, consider the types of content that thrive on Facebook. While it's a multimedia platform, video content, especially live videos, often receives higher engagement rates and broader reach. This doesn't mean you should ignore other forms of content; rather, integrate videos into a diverse content strategy that also includes thought-provoking status updates, high-quality images, and interactive polls. Each content type serves a purpose, whether it's driving engagement, providing value, or sparking conversations among your audience.

Engagement on Facebook is not just beneficial; it's crucial. The algorithm favors content that sparks conversations and meaningful interactions among users. To this end, crafting posts that encourage your audience to comment, share, and react is paramount. Pose questions, share relatable experiences, and create content that resonates on a personal level with your audience. Remember, the more your audience interacts with your content, the more your content will be prioritized by the algorithm.

Another vital component of Facebook's algorithm is the timeliness of posts. The algorithm is more likely to prioritize content that is recent and thus more relevant to users. This emphasizes the importance of knowing when your audience is most active on Facebook. Use insights and analytics to determine these peak times and schedule your posts accordingly. This ensures your content has the best chance of being seen and engaged with by your audience.

Lastly, don't underestimate the power of Facebook Groups. These can be invaluable for building a community around your brand or niche. Groups foster a sense of belonging and significantly higher levels of engagement than public pages. They are a sanctuary for like-minded individuals to share experiences, advice, and feedback. When leveraged correctly, Groups can amplify your reach, enhance brand loyalty, and even provide insight into your audience's needs and preferences. Remember, success on Facebook is not just about broadcasting your message but about fostering genuine connections and interactions that resonate with your audience.

Instagram has cemented itself as a juggernaut in the social media landscape, being a particularly visual platform, it presents a unique blend of opportunities and challenges for those aiming to go viral and monetize their presence. This section delves into the pivotal tactics and nuanced strategies vital for mastering Instagram and leveraging its algorithm to your advantage.

The essence of Instagram's allure lies in its visual storytelling capabilities. Photos and videos are the heartbeats of successful accounts. Crafting content that is not only eye-catching but also resonates with your audience requires a deep understanding of both your niche and the kind of visuals that captivate. High-quality, engaging visuals, coupled with compelling captions that encourage interaction, can significantly enhance your content's reach and engagement, propelling your growth on the platform.

Understanding and navigating the Instagram algorithm is another crucial facet to unlock exponential growth. The algorithm favors content that generates high engagement rates soon after posting. Utilize insights and analytics to determine the best times to post, ensuring your content is seen by as many of your followers as possible. Additionally, leveraging features like Instagram Stories, Reels, and IGTV can aid in increasing visibility and engagement, courtesy of Instagram's push to showcase these formats.

Hashtags and collaborations present yet another tier of strategy for amplifying your Instagram presence. A well-researched hashtag strategy can place your content in front of relevant audiences beyond your current followers, potentially boosting visibility and engagement. Similarly, collaborations with other creators or brands can introduce your profile to wider audiences. It's about finding synergies with partners whose followers might find your content valuable or engaging.

Lastly, staying up-to-date with Instagram's ever-evolving features and adjusting your strategy accordingly is essential. Whether it's changes in the algorithm, the introduction of new content formats, or shifts in user behavior and preferences, your ability to adapt swiftly can make a significant difference. Engaging with your community, encouraging feedback, and continuously experimenting with different content types and formats can provide insights into what works best, helping you refine your strategy for sustained growth and success on Instagram.

YouTube Transitioning into the realm of YouTube, it is crucial to understand that this platform's dynamic is vastly different from others. This differentiation is mainly due to its heavy reliance on video content, which demands a unique strategic approach. YouTube isn't just another social media platform; it's the second largest search engine in the world, right behind Google. A sound strategy for YouTube involves not only crafting content that resonates with your audience but also ensuring it is discoverable.

Firstly, understanding YouTube's algorithm is key. This platform recommends videos to users based on their viewing habits, making it essential to optimize your content. Use descriptive titles, detailed descriptions filled with relevant keywords, and custom thumbnails that grab attention. These elements work in tandem to improve your video's visibility and click-through rate. Remember, on YouTube, engagement (likes, comments, and shares) along with watch time influences how your content ranks and, consequently, how often it is recommended to viewers. This fosters a cycle where good content gets more visibility, leading to more engagement and still greater visibility. Therefore, prioritizing content that keeps viewers watching for longer periods can significantly impact your growth on YouTube.

Developing a content calendar for YouTube can be a game-changer. Since consistency is a major growth factor, planning your posts ahead of time ensures a steady stream of content, keeping your audience engaged and attracting new viewers. This approach helps you to stay ahead, providing ample time to create high-quality videos that provide value. Whether you are aiming to entertain, educate, or inspire, ensuring your videos are well-produced and bring something unique to the table is paramount.

Interacting with your audience on YouTube also can't be overlooked. Responding to comments, asking viewers to engage with content by liking and subscribing, and even incorporating viewer suggestions into your content can bolster community feeling. Hosting live sessions and Q&A segments can further deepen your connection with your audience, making them feel valued and part of a larger community. This level of engagement transforms viewers into loyal subscribers who are more likely to share your content, fueling organic growth.

Lastly, leveraging YouTube analytics is instrumental in fine-tuning your strategy. Analytics provide insights into who your viewers are, what they like to watch, and how they discover your videos. Such data helps in making informed decisions about future content and strategies for promoting your videos on and beyond YouTube. Paying attention to metrics such as watch time, audience retention, and traffic sources can uncover trends and patterns, guiding you in optimizing both current and future content for success. As with any social media platform, adapting and evolving based on analytics is crucial to staying ahead in the ever-competitive landscape of YouTube.

Adjusting Your Strategy Based on Analytics

Mastering the algorithm is akin to mastering a constantly evolving puzzle. Every piece represents a different facet of your strategy, impacted by countless variables that change with the landscape of social media. At the heart of these strategies, analytics serve as your compass, guiding your decisions and adjustments for optimal growth. In this section, we dive deep into leveraging analytics to refine your approach, ensuring your content doesn't just speak to your audience but resonates with them.

First off, understanding the basics of analytics is crucial. Social media platforms offer insights that range from superficial to complex. Engagement rates, follower growth, and content reach give you an overview, while deeper metrics like audience demographics, content interaction times, and behaviors paint a more nuanced picture. These numbers aren't just figures; they're the reflection of your audience's preferences, habits, and responses to your content.

Initiating this analytics-driven approach begins with setting clear, measurable goals. What are you aiming to achieve? Increased engagement, higher conversion rates, or expanded reach? Your goals will dictate the metrics you need to focus on, shaping a strategy that's geared towards achieving specific outcomes rather than shooting in the dark.

Once goals are set, it's time to dive into the data. Start simple by observing patterns in your most and least successful posts. What differentiates them? Is it the content type, posting time, or perhaps the tone of voice? This preliminary analysis will provide initial insights on adjustments needed to enhance your content's performance.

Effectively adjusting your content strategy based on analytics requires regular monitoring and flexibility. As you experiment with different content types, posting schedules, and engagement strategies, keep a close eye on how these changes influence your key metrics. It's crucial to adopt a test-and-learn mindset, where every piece of content is an opportunity to learn more about your audience's preferences.

Engagement analytics are particularly telling. Look beyond likes and followers; analyze comments, shares, and the nature of interactions. Are your audiences actively participating in discussions? Do they share your content within their networks? Understanding these behaviors will provide valuable insights into the type of content that fosters community and conversation.

Don't underestimate the power of demographic analytics either. Knowing the age, location, and interests of your audience can significantly refine your content strategy. Tailoring your content to match the cultural and regional preferences of your audience can enhance relatability and engagement.

Timing is another aspect where analytics play a crucial role. Most platforms provide data on when your audience is most active. Aligning your posting schedule with these peak times can drastically increase your content's visibility and engagement.

Analytics also guide strategic decisions beyond content creation. They can inform your promotional strategies, indicating which content types might benefit from paid promotion or which demographics to target in ad campaigns. This approach ensures your budget is used efficiently, maximizing ROI on promotional activities.

Collaboration opportunities can also be uncovered through careful analysis. By identifying accounts that your audience engages with, you can pinpoint potential partners who align with your brand's ethos and appeal to your target audience, leveraging cross-promotion to expand your reach.

As you refine your strategy, documentation is key. Keep detailed records of the adjustments made and their outcomes. This not only helps in identifying successful strategies but also in understanding the evolving patterns of your audience's behavior over time.

Critical to this analytics-driven approach is the willingness to pivot. Social media is fluid, and what works today might not work tomorrow. Staying attuned to the shifting tides, ready to adjust your sails as needed, is paramount. This agility enables you to stay ahead of changes, whether they're in audience behavior, platform algorithms, or broader social trends.

Lastly, remember that analytics are a tool, not a rulebook. They provide guidance and insights, but the human element—creativity, empathy, and genuine connection—should not be overshadowed by numbers. Balancing data-driven strategies with authentic content creation is the key to truly mastering the algorithm and connecting with your audience on a deeper level.

In conclusion, adjusting your strategy based on analytics isn't just about reacting to numbers; it's about actively engaging with the story those numbers tell. This approach empowers you to craft more resonant content, build a stronger community, and propel your growth on social media platforms. The algorithm might be a complex beast, but with analytics as your guide, you'll be well-equipped to master it.

Remember, the landscape of social media is always evolving. As you continue to adapt and adjust your strategy, lean into the insights that analytics offer, but never lose sight of the core purpose of your social media presence—to connect, engage, and inspire your audience.

Chapter 4:
Growth Hacking Techniques

As we pivot from mastering algorithms to actively propelling our social media platforms into the stratosphere, growth hacking emerges as the secret sauce to viral success. Imagine leveraging creative, low-cost strategies to exponentially grow your followers and drive engagement. It's about smartly using hashtags, not just throwing them out there, but understanding the art behind their power to make your content discoverable. But it doesn't stop there. Collaboration and cross-promotion are your allies, allowing you to tap into new audiences by partnering with others who share your vision. And who can resist the allure of contests and giveaways? These are not just tricks but strategic moves that create buzz and incentivize engagement. In this chapter, we'll dissect these techniques, piecing together how each can be a game-changer for anyone looking to not just grow, but explode on social media. Each tactic, when executed with precision, can open floodgates to a torrent of followers, likes, and shares, setting the stage for viral success and, ultimately, monetization.

The Art of Hashtags

Continuing from mastering the platforms, now it's time to delve into the science and art combined in using hashtags effectively—a cornerstone strategy in your growth hacking toolkit. Hashtags, those ubiquitous symbols followed by keywords or phrases, significantly expand the reach and visibility of your content across social media. They function as clickable links, guiding users to a pool of content sharing a theme or topic. Mastering their use can catalyze your growth exponentially, but it demands more than just slapping popular tags on your posts.

First, understand that each social media platform has its unique environment and rules of engagement with hashtags. Instagram, for example, allows up to 30 hashtags per post, but that doesn't mean you should necessarily use the maximum limit. Twitter, with its character count constraint, pushes for more concise and potent hashtag use. The key here is balance and relevance—the golden rules for hashtagging. Start with researching top-performing hashtags within your niche, which are broad enough to attract a wide audience but specific enough to target those truly interested in your content.

Creating a blend of broad, niche-specific, and brand-specific hashtags can set your content apart. Brand hashtags are particularly potent as they cultivate a sense of community and belonging among your audience, making them more likely to engage with your content and share it. They're the cornerstone of any viral campaign, acting as a rallying cry for your followers and an easy way for new audiences to discover your content.

Timing and trends are also critical when it comes to hashtags. Leveraging trending hashtags can throw your content into the viral vortex, but relevance is key. Jumping on a trending hashtag that doesn't align with your brand or message can do more harm than good. Monitoring tools and social media analytics can help you identify which hashtags are trending within your audience segment or industry, allowing you to participate authentically in larger conversations.

Localization of hashtags is another underutilized strategy. If your brand or content has a geographic focus, local hashtags can help you reach a targeted audience that's more likely to engage with your content. These tags can range from city names, local event names, or local trends. Coupled with generic hashtags, they enhance your visibility to a community that's within reach and interested in local content.

Hashtag challenges and campaigns are another avenue for growth. Encouraging your followers to use a specific hashtag in their posts can generate buzz and enhance engagement. This peer-to-peer recommendation system not only broadens your reach but also solidifies your community, as participants see their content shared and celebrated by the brand and fellow community members.

Analytics play a key role in refining your hashtag strategy. Most social media platforms offer insights into how your hashtags are performing in terms of reach and engagement. Studying these analytics allows you to continuously adjust and refine your strategy, cutting out low-performing tags and doubling down on those that are effective. Remember, the social media landscape is ever-evolving, and so should your hashtag strategy.

Consistency in your hashtag usage also aids in building brand recall. By regularly using a set of core hashtags, especially those unique to your brand, you make it easier for your audience to remember and use them. This practice is critical in cultivating an engaged and loyal community that actively participates in spreading your content through their networks.

Lastly, it's important to remember that hashtags are just one part of a broader social media strategy. They are powerful tools for growth and engagement but work best when used in conjunction with high-quality content, engagement strategies, and other growth hacking techniques. Think of hashtags as the spices in your social media recipe—they can enhance the dish, but they can't make up for poor-quality ingredients.

In summary, mastering the art of hashtags requires a blend of research, creativity, and strategic thinking. By staying informed about best practices and continuously adapting your approach, you can leverage hashtags to significantly boost your social media presence, engagement, and growth. Remember, the goal is not just to go viral but to create a lasting impact and build a loyal community around your brand.

Collaboration and Cross-Promotion

By now, we've explored the cornerstone strategies of setting up your social media profiles, mastering the algorithm, and creating content that resonates. But there's a powerful catalyst that can exponentially amplify your reach: collaboration and cross-promotion. Let's delve into how partnering with others in your niche or complementary fields can accelerate your growth and open new avenues for visibility.

Collaboration is not just about sharing audiences; it's about creating a synergy that benefits all parties involved. When two or more creators or brands come together, they bring their unique strengths to the table, potentially creating content that's more engaging and far-reaching than what they could achieve individually. This synergy can take many forms, from joint live streams and interviews to featuring in each other's posts or videos.

Getting started with collaboration might seem daunting at first. Begin by identifying potential partners who share a similar audience but aren't direct competitors. Think about what unique value you can offer to them and their audience. It's important to approach potential partners with a clear proposal that outlines the mutual benefits of collaborating. Remember, it's not just about what you can gain but what you can contribute.

Cross-promotion, a subset of collaboration, involves promoting each other's content across different platforms. This technique is particularly effective because it introduces your brand to a wholly new—yet relevant—audience. But cross-promotion calls for a strategic approach. You'll want to ensure that the content being promoted aligns with your brand values and resonates with your audience to maintain authenticity.

Creating a collaboration agreement, even if it's informal, can set clear expectations for both parties. This agreement should outline content deliverables, timelines, and how the results of the collaboration will be measured. Keeping track of analytics and performance metrics is crucial for understanding the impact of your joint efforts and how they could be improved in the future.

One challenge you might face is finding the right collaboration partners. Social media platforms themselves can be excellent tools for discovery. Engage with potential collaborators by commenting on their posts or sharing their content, building a relationship before pitching a collaboration. Networking events, both online and offline, also offer great opportunities to connect with like-minded individuals and brands.

Leverage tools and apps designed to facilitate collaboration. Platforms such as Collabstr or Upfluence can help connect influencers and brands, making it easier to find partnerships that align with your niche. Utilizing these resources can streamline the process and introduce you to potential partners you might not have discovered otherwise.

Once you've launched a collaboration, promoting it effectively is key. Utilize all your social media channels to share the collaboration, encouraging your audience to check out your partner's content. This multi-platform approach ensures maximum visibility and engagement. Don't forget to monitor and engage with comments and feedback from both your and your partner's audiences; this direct engagement can further boost your reach.

While collaborations can offer significant rewards, they also come with risks, particularly when it comes to brand alignment. Take the time to vet potential partners thoroughly. Ensure their content and audience demographics align closely with yours. A partnership that seems beneficial on the surface but doesn't align with your brand's values or audience's interests can do more harm than good.

Setting realistic goals for your collaboration is crucial. Whether it's increasing your follower count, boosting engagement on a specific type of content, or driving sales, having clear objectives will guide your collaborative efforts and make measuring success easier. Be transparent with your collaboration partners about these goals to ensure everyone is working toward the same targets.

Innovative collaboration formats can help your content stand out. While guest posts or takeovers are popular options, think outside the box with formats like joint webinars, co-hosted challenges, or collaborative giveaways. These unique formats can generate heightened interest and engagement from both audiences.

The post-collaboration period is just as important as the collaboration itself. Take the time to review the results of your collaborative efforts. Analyze the data to understand what worked well and what could be improved. This evaluation is essential not just for measuring success but for learning and refining your approach to future collaborations.

Furthermore, view each collaboration as a building block for long-term relationships. After a successful collaboration, keep the lines of communication open for potential future projects. These ongoing partnerships can compound in value over time, creating a network of allies that can help amplify your content and grow your presence on social media.

Finally, always express gratitude. A thank-you note or shoutout to your collaborators not only strengthens your relationship but also sets a positive tone for potential future projects. Acknowledge the collective effort it takes to make collaborations successful, fostering a culture of mutual support and appreciation.

In conclusion, collaboration and cross-promotion are dynamic tools that, when executed thoughtfully, can significantly enhance your social media growth and influence. By engaging with like-minded individuals and brands, leveraging your combined strengths, and creatively promoting one another, you can unlock new levels of visibility and engagement. Remember, the key to effective collaboration is mutual benefit, authenticity, and alignment with your core brand values.

Contests and Giveaways

Let's dive into one of the most engaging growth hacking techniques that can significantly broaden your social media horizons: contests and giveaways. These are not just throwaway strategies; when executed thoughtfully, they can amplify your reach, boost engagement, and even skyrocket your follower count overnight. The mechanism is simple—people love free stuff. But the art of deploying contests and giveaways effectively is where the real magic lies.

First things first, you've got to plan your contest with a clear objective in mind. Are you aiming to increase your followers, generate leads, or perhaps drive more traffic to your website? Your goal dictates the structure of your contest. For instance, if you're looking to boost followers, you might ask participants to follow your account, like a post, and tag a friend in the comments to enter. The beauty of this strategy is its simplicity and the domino effect it generates in terms of reach and engagement.

Choosing the right prize is crucial. It must be compelling enough to entice your target audience to participate. Remember, the prize doesn't have to break the bank; sometimes, exclusivity or early access to your products or services can be just as appealing as a high-value item. The key is ensuring relevancy to your brand and your audience's interests, which maintains the quality of new followers or leads you gain.

Transparency is paramount. Clearly communicate the rules, the criteria for winning, and how and when the winner will be selected. Using a random winner generator not only simplifies the selection process but also adds a layer of fairness and transparency. Make sure to announce the winner publicly and consider sharing a follow-up post that showcases them enjoying their prize, which adds legitimacy to your contest and encourages participation in future giveaways.

Promotion of your contest cannot be an afterthought. Utilize all your social media channels, even those not directly involved in the contest, to spread the word. Tailor your promotion strategy to fit the specifics of each platform. For instance, Stories can be a great way to keep your audience engaged and reminded of the contest, while a pinned tweet might be your best bet on Twitter.

Partnerships can elevate the reach of your contest exponentially. Teaming up with influencers or brands that share a similar target audience can introduce your profile to users who are likely to be genuinely interested in your content. Such collaborations can also add credibility to your contest and increase the perceived value of the prizes.

Leverage user-generated content to your advantage. Encouraging participants to create content as part of the entry process, such as sharing photos featuring your product, not only provides you with valuable promotional material but also increases engagement and personal investment in the contest's outcome from participants.

Analyze and learn from each contest. Use analytics tools to track participation, engagement, and follower growth. Understand what worked and what didn't, which will allow you to refine your strategy for future promotions. Pay attention to feedback from your audience and be ready to adapt your approach accordingly.

Finally, contests and giveaways should not be standalone tactics but integrated elements of your broader social media strategy. They are fantastic for gaining immediate attention, but sustaining that growth requires consistent engagement, quality content, and strategies that build genuine relationships with your audience.

Remember, the ultimate aim of contests and giveaways is not just to increase numbers but to foster a more engaged, loyal community around your brand. By offering real value, maintaining transparency, and continually optimizing your approach, you'll not only grow your social media presence but create a vibrant, active, and engaged community.

Chapter 5:
Going Viral

In the realm of social media, 'going viral' is often seen as the holy grail for content creators. It's that pivotal moment when your content breaks beyond your usual audience, catching the attention of millions worldwide. But what's the secret sauce? It's not just about happenstance; there's a science behind it. The essence of virality lies in crafting content that resonates on a human level, content that's so relatable, amusing, or intriguing that people can't resist sharing it. While we've touched on understanding your audience and the algorithm in previous chapters, it's crucial now to leverage that insight to create content with the potential to go viral. This means paying close attention to trends and current events, making your content timely and irresistible. However, it's also about authenticity—your content should still align with your brand's voice and mission, ensuring that when you do go viral, it's meaningful and contributes to your social media empire's growth. Remember, virality isn't just about views or likes; it's about amplifying your message in a way that connects and sticks with your audience long after the buzz has faded.

The Science Behind Virality

In the landscape of social media, going viral is often seen as striking digital gold. But what's often missed is that there's a science to it. It's not just about luck or being at the right place at the right time. There are patterns, mechanisms, and psychological triggers behind why content spreads like wildfire. Understanding the science behind virality is your first step in crafting content with the potential to take off.

At its core, virality is about human emotions and psychology. Content that evokes strong emotions, whether it's joy, surprise, or even anger, tends to be shared more. It's because when we feel something deeply, we're more likely to want to share that experience with others. It's a form of social currency. This is why videos of heartwarming reunions or outrage-inducing incidents can rack up millions of views seemingly overnight.

Another vital aspect of virality is the element of value. Whether it's educational content, entertaining videos, or problem-solving posts, if your audience finds real value in what you're sharing, they're more likely to pass it on. People share content that they believe will be useful, interesting, or entertaining to others in their network. It's about making the sharer look good in the eyes of their peers.

Let's not forget about the role of timing. The digital world is always on, and trends can come and go in the blink of an eye. Being able to quickly leverage trending topics or current events can act as a catalyst for virality. The timing of your content plays a crucial role in its potential to go viral. It's about riding the wave, not creating it from scratch.

Another critical factor is simplicity and relatability. The easier it is for people to digest and relate to your content, the more likely it is to be shared. Complex or niche content can have a dedicated audience, but its virality potential is often limited. Content that's simple, relatable, and easy to understand has a broader appeal, increasing its shareability.

Networking also plays a significant role in the spread of viral content. Building relationships with influencers and other content creators can help your content reach a wider audience faster. A share or mention from a well-known personality in your niche can set the ball rolling towards virality.

Understanding social sharing triggers is paramount. People share content for various reasons - to inform, entertain, express themselves, connect with others, or even to support causes they care about. Tapping into these desires can help you create content that people are more inclined to share. It's about aligning your content with the motives behind social sharing.

The role of platforms cannot be overstated. Each social media platform has its quirks and algorithms. Tailoring your content to fit the preferences of each platform increases its chances of going viral. What works on Instagram might not work on Twitter. Understanding the nuances of each platform is key.

Engagement is another critical factor. Content that sparks conversation and encourages interaction tends to perform better in terms of virality. When your audience engages with your content, it signals the algorithms that your content is valuable, pushing it to more users and increasing its virality potential.

However, it's important to measure and adapt. Relying solely on virality without understanding its impact can be misleading. It's essential to track the right metrics and analyze whether your viral content is helping you meet your larger objectives. Sometimes, viral content can bring in a lot of attention but not necessarily the right kind of engagement or conversions.

Incorporating storytelling into your content can also enhance its viral potential. Humans are naturally drawn to stories. They are more memorable and impactful. Content that tells a story, whether it's through a single post, video, or a series of content pieces, can resonate more deeply with your audience, making it more shareable.

It's also worth noting the unexpected. Sometimes virality happens spontaneously, triggered by something seemingly trivial or unexpected. While you can't plan for these moments, being adaptable and ready to leverage unexpected opportunities when they arise is crucial.

Experimentation and creativity are your best tools. The digital landscape is always evolving, and so are the tastes and preferences of online audiences. What went viral yesterday might not work today. Consistently experimenting with different types of content and creative approaches is vital in finding what resonates best with your audience.

In conclusion, while the idea of going viral is enticing, it's a complex process that requires understanding the underlying factors that drive social sharing. By tapping into human emotions, providing value, timing your content right, and leveraging the unique features of each social media platform, you can increase your chances of creating content that not only goes viral but also helps you achieve your larger goals. Remember, virality is not an end in itself but a means to grow, engage, and monetize your social media presence effectively.

Lastly, always keep your audience at the center of your content creation process. Understanding what they like, dislike, and what drives them to share can provide invaluable insights into creating not just viral content, but content that truly matters. It's about striking a balance between capturing the moment and staying true to your brand and message. This, in essence, is the science behind virality.

Crafting Content with Viral Potential

In the whirlwind world of social media, crafting content that has the potential to go viral is akin to capturing lightning in a bottle. It's an amalgamation of art, science, and a dash of serendipity. But don't let the unpredictability deter you. With the right approach, you can tilt the odds in your favor and significantly increase your chances of creating that breakout post or video.

First and foremost, understanding the psychological drivers behind sharing content is crucial. People share content that evokes strong emotional reactions, such as joy, amusement, surprise, or even righteous anger. Content that elicits these feelings has a better chance of being passed along and becoming viral. This means that when you're brainstorming content ideas, think deeply about the emotional chord you're aiming to strike in your audience.

Another key factor in creating viral-worthy content is relatability. The more people can see themselves or their experiences in your content, the more likely they are to share it. This doesn't mean you can't explore unique or niche topics. On the contrary, showcasing unusual or specific experiences in a relatable manner can make your content stand out.

Don't underestimate the power of storytelling. A well-crafted narrative can turn a simple post into a compelling saga that people feel compelled to share with their own networks. Whether it's a short anecdote or a multi-part series, stories have the power to connect with people on a personal level and leave a lasting impression.

Timing also plays a critical role in viral content. Aligning your posts with trending topics, current events, or seasonal themes can give your content an extra boost by tapping into the collective consciousness of your audience. However, timing isn't just about what you post, but when you post. Pay attention to your analytics to identify when your audience is most active and schedule your potential viral content accordingly.

In the realm of viral content, originality cannot be overstated. With millions of posts circulating on social media every day, standing out requires a fresh take or a new perspective. This doesn't mean every post must be groundbreaking, but adding your unique twist to prevailing trends can make all the difference.

Visuals are your best friend when it comes to viral content. Eye-catching photos, compelling videos, and creative graphics have a higher chance of stopping someone in their scroll and engaging them. Investing time and resources into high-quality visuals can dramatically elevate the shareability of your content.

Interactive content, such as polls, quizzes, and challenges, invites your audience to engage on a deeper level. This not only increases the likelihood of your content being shared but also fosters a sense of community among your followers. Engagement breeds engagement, setting the stage for virality.

Don't shy away from leveraging the power of influencers. A nod, share, or collaboration with a well-followed influencer can catapult your content into the viral stratosphere. However, it's important to collaborate with influencers whose audience aligns with your own for maximum impact.

Creating viral content also means being prepared for the aftermath. Ensure your profiles and systems are ready to handle increased traffic and engagement. This preparation includes having a clear call to action, optimizing your profiles for new followers, and having a plan to capitalize on the spotlight.

Remember, virality is fleeting. While one viral post can give you a significant boost, sustained effort and consistency are what build empires. Use the momentum from viral hits to bolster your overall content strategy, keeping your audience engaged and attracting new followers.

Analytics are your roadmap. After each campaign or content push, dive deep into your analytics to understand what worked and what didn't. This data is invaluable for refining your approach and increasing your chances of going viral in the future.

Finally, keep experimenting. The landscape of social media is ever-changing, and what goes viral one day may not the next. Stay curious, keep testing different types of content, and adapt based on what resonates with your audience and the broader social media community.

At the end of the day, crafting content with viral potential is both a science and an art. It requires insight into human psychology, a deep understanding of social media dynamics, and a healthy dose of creativity. By focusing on emotional impact, timing, originality, and engagement, you're setting the stage for content that not only goes viral but also leaves a lasting impact.

While there's no guaranteed formula for virality, approaching content creation with these principles in mind will significantly enhance your chances of capturing the internet's fleeting attention. Remember, each post is an opportunity to capture lightning in a bottle – with the right strategy, your next viral hit could be just around the corner.

Leveraging Trends and Current Events

In an online world that moves at the speed of light, keeping your finger on the pulse of current events and trending topics can transform a routine content calendar into a dynamite strategy for viral success. It's like catching the perfect wave; by aligning your content with what's already capturing the public's imagination, you greatly increase your visibility and relevance. However, navigating this landscape requires finesse, strategic thinking, and, most importantly, authenticity.

First and foremost, it's key to stay informed. This means going beyond just knowing the top trends on Twitter or the latest memes on

Instagram. Delve into the stories behind the headlines. Understand why they're capturing public interest and how they resonate with your audience. This deeper level of insight will enable you to craft content that doesn't just ride the trend but adds value to the conversation.

However, it's not just about jumping on every bandwagon. Not all trends or current events will align with your brand voice or mission. It's essential to select those that resonate with your established identity and values. Authenticity here is crucial. Your audience can spot insincerity from a mile away, and nothing can damage trust quicker than appearing to exploit a situation for views or likes. So, when you do find a trend that aligns with your brand, dive in with genuine enthusiasm and a unique perspective.

One effective strategy is to create content that educates your audience about the trend or event. This could be a deep dive into the origins of a viral challenge, an analysis of why a certain hashtag is trending, or a breakdown of the key players in a current news story. By providing context and insight, you establish your brand as a knowledgeable and reliable source of information.

Another approach is to offer a fresh take or an unconventional angle on a trending topic. This could mean creating a parody, offering expert commentary, or presenting a counter-argument to the prevailing narrative. The goal is to stand out in a crowded field and give your audience a reason to share your content.

Engaging directly with trends through interactive content can also be a powerful tool. Polls, quizzes, and challenges invite your audience to participate in the conversation, not just consume your content. This creates a sense of community and involvement that can amplify the reach of your posts.

It's also worth considering the timing of your content. In the world of social media, timing can be everything. A perfectly timed post that taps into the zeitgeist can catapult your brand into viral territory. This requires not just awareness of trends but the agility to create and publish content quickly and efficiently.

Don't overlook the power of hashtags. When used strategically, they can increase the discoverability of your content and link your posts to larger conversations. But beware of hashtag overkill. Choose a few relevant ones that enhance rather than clutter your message.

Collaborating with influencers who are known for staying on top of trends can also boost your brand's visibility. Their endorsement can lend credibility to your content and introduce your brand to new audiences. It's a symbiotic relationship that, when executed with care, can lead to mutually beneficial viral success.

Visual content, especially videos, often has a higher likelihood of going viral. If a picture is worth a thousand words, a video can tell a full story, especially when it captures the essence of a current trend or event. Investing time in creating compelling video content can pay off dividends in terms of engagement and shareability.

Monitoring the performance of your trend-based content is essential for refining your strategy. Use analytics to track which types of posts resonate most with your audience and which platforms give you the best reach. This data can guide your future content decisions and help you hone in on the most effective ways to leverage trends.

Remember, the goal of leveraging trends and current events isn't just to get a quick boost in views. It's about building lasting relationships with your audience by consistently providing value and relevance. It's this long-term commitment to quality and engagement that ultimately leads to sustained viral success.

In conclusion, successfully leveraging trends and current events in your social media strategy requires a careful balance of awareness, authenticity, and agility. By staying informed, choosing the right trends to engage with, and creating content that resonates and adds value, you can ride the wave of viral success to new heights. Always keep your audience's interests and needs at the forefront, and never lose sight of the soul of your brand. With these guiding principles, you're well on your way to transforming current buzz into lasting impact.

Chapter 6:
Engagement: The Key to Growth

Just walking through the blueprint of viral success, we've seen the role of content, algorithms, and the fleeting excitement of going viral. Now, let's dive into the crux of growing a social media empire: engagement. Imagine engagement as the heartbeat of your social media presence—without it, your content, no matter how brilliant, exists in a vacuum. The essence of this chapter leans heavily on not just sparking but nurturing engagement, transforming passive observers into an active, committed community. This pivot from mere viewership to active engagement hinges on strategies like prompting your audience to share their thoughts through comments, leveraging the dynamism of live sessions to connect in real time, and meticulously crafting posts that invite shares. It's not just about broadcasting your message into the digital expanse; it's about creating a feedback loop where your audience feels seen, heard, and valued. Through this, engagement transcends being a mere metric, embodying instead the foundational pillar supporting the monumental structure of social media success.

Building Genuine Connections

After laying a solid foundation and mastering content creation, the next crucial step to growth on social media is building genuine connections. Stepping into this sphere requires more than just broadcasting your messages; it's about creating a two-way conversation with your audience. It's the difference between talking at someone versus talking with them.

To initiate these connections, start by understanding your audience deeply. This means going beyond demographics. You need to know what excites them, what challenges they face, and what content resonates with them most. When you begin to understand these nuances, your interactions become more meaningful and your content more impactful.

Engagement isn't just about responding to comments or messages; it's about listening. True listening involves observing the overall sentiment of your audience, paying attention to trending topics, and even noting what they're not saying explicitly. This insight allows you to create content that matters to them, fostering a deeper connection.

Another essential aspect of building genuine connections is consistency. This doesn't only pertain to how often you post but also to your voice and brand. People resonate with authenticity. They want to follow and engage with someone who is real and relatable. Let your personality shine through in every post, story, and interaction.

Storytelling is a powerful tool in your arsenal. Narratives have been a way for humans to connect and share experiences for millennia. Share stories of your journey, the behind-the-scenes of your process, and the challenges you face. It makes you approachable, relatable, and memorable.

Another tactic is to leverage user-generated content. When your audience shares their stories, photos, or experiences related to your brand, repost them. It not only shows that you value their contribution but also encourages others to share their experiences, creating a sense of community around your brand.

Hosting live sessions can also significantly boost your efforts in building genuine connections. Live video offers real-time engagement, allowing for spontaneous questions and answers, which can lead to more profound and meaningful interactions. It's an effective way to show your audience the person behind the brand, in an unedited and authentic setting.

Collaborations are equally vital. Partner with peers in your industry or complementary fields to tap into a new audience. This exposes your brand to people likely to be interested in your content but haven't discovered you yet. Choose partners who align with your brand values to maintain authenticity.

Feedback is a treasure trove of insights. Ask for it explicitly, through polls, questions, or direct messages. This not only provides you with valuable information to improve but also makes your followers feel heard and valued. Acting on this feedback demonstrates that you prioritize their experience and satisfaction.

Don't forget the power of gratitude. A simple thank you goes a long way in humanizing your online presence. Acknowledge the support, shares, and comments. Personalized thank-you messages, shoutouts, or even small rewards for loyal followers can significantly enhance loyalty and advocacy for your brand.

Equally important is the principle of reciprocity. Engage with your followers' content, not just when they interact with yours. Visit their profiles, like their posts, and leave meaningful comments. This not only strengthens relationships but also fosters a community where engagement is mutual.

Challenges and contests can spark excitement and participation among your followers. Create challenges that are fun and easy to participate in, with incentives that are valuable to your audience. This not only boosts interaction but also allows your followers to contribute to your content in creative ways.

Keep in mind the importance of patience and persistence. Building genuine connections takes time. It's about slowly weaving a fabric of trust, respect, and mutual support. There will be ups and downs, but staying committed to genuinely engaging with your audience will yield profound, lasting relationships.

Lastly, always be adapting. The digital landscape and your audience's preferences will evolve. Stay curious and open to change, experimenting with new formats, platforms, and strategies for engagement. What works today might not work tomorrow, so the willingness to pivot is essential. This dynamic approach will keep your connections fresh and growing.

In summary, building genuine connections on social media is multifaceted - involving listening, consistency, storytelling, collaboration, and engagement. By adopting these practices, you're not just growing your following; you're cultivating a community that values and supports your brand. Remember, at the heart of social media success is the power of human connection.

Strategies for Increasing Engagement

In the quest to unlock the full potential of your social media platform, it's crucial we focus on ramping up engagement. Engagement is the lifeblood of social media success. It's not just about gathering followers; it's about kindling an actively participating community that's keen on what you have to say, share, and offer. So, how do we turn passive followers into enthusiastic participants? Let's dive into some actionable strategies.

First and foremost, the quality of your content cannot be understated. It goes beyond just posting regularly. Each piece of content should serve a purpose, whether it's to educate, entertain, inspire, or provoke thought. Think about what your audience will find valuable and invest time in creating content that resonates with this. High-quality content encourages more shares, comments, and interactions by default.

Understanding the power of questions is next. Encourage your followers to voice their opinions by asking open-ended questions related to your post. This not only boosts engagement rates but also provides you with valuable insights into your audience's preferences and thoughts. Remember, it's a two-way conversation; actively respond to the comments to keep the dialogue going.

Another key aspect is to personalize your interactions. People crave genuine connections, and showing that there's a real person behind the social media account can make a huge difference. Addressing followers by name, sharing personal stories relevant to your brand, and showing behind-the-scenes content can make your audience feel more connected to you.

Leverage the power of storytelling. Everyone loves a good story, and integrating storytelling into your posts can captivate your audience's attention. It can be something simple like the journey of creating your product, a customer's experience, or even challenges you've overcome. Stories are relatable and shareable, leading to increased engagement.

Don't underestimate the impact of visuals. Bright, eye-catching images or videos can stop a scroller in their tracks. Experiment with different types of visual content like GIFs, infographics, and short video clips to discover what your audience prefers. Visual content is more likely to be shared, increasing visibility and engagement.

Timing your posts thoughtfully can also affect engagement. Use analytics tools to find out when your followers are most active and schedule your posts accordingly. The goal is to share content when it's most likely to be seen and interacted with, giving it the best chance to generate engagement.

Incorporating polls and quizzes is a fun and easy way to encourage interaction. They're not only engaging but also a great way to gather opinions and preferences from your audience. Social media platforms like Instagram offer easy-to-use poll stickers in stories, making it convenient to get started.

Using relevant hashtags wisely can broaden your reach and attract a more engaged audience. However, it's important to use them judiciously. Too many hashtags can appear spammy. Focus on using relevant hashtags that connect your content to a broader conversation or community.

Creating exclusive content for your most active followers can foster a sense of belonging and increase loyalty. This could be in the form of behind-the-scenes content, early access to products or sales, or exclusive Q&A sessions. Making your followers feel special is a surefire way to boost engagement.

Running contests and giveaways is a proven strategy to increase engagement. Everyone loves the chance to win something. Ensure the entry criteria involve engaging with your content, such as by liking, commenting, or sharing your post. This not only boosts engagement but can also increase your follower count.

Collaborating with influencers or other brands can introduce your content to a wider audience. Choose partners whose audience overlaps with yours to ensure the content is relevant. This can lead to a significant boost in engagement as you tap into new communities.

Hosting live sessions can bring a significant engagement spike. Live sessions offer a unique opportunity for real-time interaction. Whether it's a Q&A, a behind-the-scenes look at your day, or a live tutorial, these sessions can make your audience feel more connected to you.

Finally, always analyze your engagement data. It's important to keep track of what's working and what's not. Use insights and analytics provided by social media platforms to refine your strategy continually.

Understanding your engagement patterns can help you tailor your future content for better performance.

In conclusion, increasing engagement on your social media requires a blend of creativity, authenticity, and strategic planning. By implementing these strategies, you're not just boosting numbers— you're building a community that's actively interested in your content and brand. Engagement is the cornerstone of growth in the digital world, and mastering it opens up endless possibilities for virality and success.

Encouraging Comments and Shares As we delve into the dynamics of boosting engagement on social media, it's imperative to grasp the essence of encouraging comments and shares. This isn't merely about increasing numbers but about fostering a community where dialogue and interactions are valued. Creating content that motivates your audience to engage not only amplifies your reach but also strengthens your relationship with your followers. Let's break down actionable strategies to turn passive viewers into active participants.

Firstly, ending your posts with a question is more than a tactic; it's an invitation. Questions provoke thought and prompt responses. They transform your posts from statements into conversations. Whether you're asking for opinions, experiences, or recommendations, questions make your audience feel their input is valued. This straightforward approach can significantly increase the number and quality of comments you receive.

Another powerful method is harnessing the power of storytelling. Stories evoke emotions and connect on a personal level. When you share relatable experiences, triumphs, or challenges, you're not just broadcasting information; you're inviting your audience into your world. Emotional connections are a catalyst for engagement; stories that resonate with your audience are more likely to be shared with their networks, extending your reach organically.

Let's talk about the content that encourages sharing. 'Shareable' content typically has a few characteristics: it's valuable, entertaining, or evocative. This could mean crafting insightful tips, hilarious anecdotes, or heartwarming stories. When your content strikes a chord, sharing becomes a means for your audience to express themselves or bring value to others. Encourage sharing by creating content that aligns with your audience's interests and values.

Integrating calls to action (CTAs) into your posts is also crucial. Sometimes, your audience needs a gentle nudge to take that step from viewer to participant. A CTA can be as simple as "Share if you agree!" or "Tag a friend who needs to see this." These prompts serve as direct reminders for your audience to interact with your content. However, the key is to use CTAs sparingly and strategically to avoid overwhelming your followers.

Creating interactive content is another avenue to explore. Polls, quizzes, and contests can galvanize your audience to engage. They're not just participating; they're contributing to the content's outcome. This sense of involvement can significantly boost both comments and shares. Plus, interactive content offers valuable insights into your audience's preferences and behaviors, allowing you to tailor future content more effectively.

Don't underestimate the power of responding to comments. Engagement is a two-way street. By taking the time to reply, you're acknowledging your audience's input and fostering a sense of community. This can encourage others to join the conversation and, in turn, increase the visibility of your posts through social media algorithms.

Incorporating user-generated content (UGC) can also stimulate engagement. Sharing content created by your followers accomplishes two things: it shows appreciation for your community, and it encourages others to share their own experiences or creations with the hope of being featured. UGC not only diversifies your content but also builds a more inclusive and engaged community.

Lastly, understanding the nuances of each platform is vital. What works on Instagram may not resonate on Twitter. Tailoring your engagement strategies to the specific features and user behaviors of each platform can optimize your results. Whether it's leveraging Instagram Stories for polls or threading comments on Twitter for a deeper discussion, platform-specific tactics are essential in your engagement toolkit.

Encouraging comments and shares is about sparking a dialogue and building a community around your content. It's a blend of art and science, requiring creativity, authenticity, and strategic planning. By implementing these strategies, you're not just seeking growth; you're cultivating an engaged and loyal following that will be the foundation of your social media presence.

Hosting Live Sessions As we dive into the nitty-gritty of ramping up your social media engagement, we can't overlook the power of live sessions. Riding the wave of real-time interaction isn't just about showing your face; it's about crafting moments with your audience that are unreplicated and undeniably magnetic. Let's break down the strategies that can not only boost your visibility but also fortify those crucial connections with your community.

First and foremost, consistency is key. Imagine live sessions as your very own broadcast channel. Just as viewers tune in at the same time each week for their favorite TV show, your audience will begin to look forward to your live sessions. Decide on a schedule that's realistic for you and stick to it. Whether it's once a week or bi-weekly, let your audience know when to expect you live. This predictability builds anticipation and forms a habit for your viewers.

Next, let's talk content. In the live arena, the value you provide is paramount. Brainstorm session themes that are relevant to both your niche and the real-time interests of your audience. Are there trending topics you can discuss? Can you offer a live tutorial or Q&A session that addresses common questions or concerns? The aim is to deliver content that's not just engaging but also directly beneficial to those tuning in.

Interaction is the heart of live sessions. Encourage viewers to submit questions or share their thoughts, and make it a point to acknowledge their contributions during the broadcast. This two-way exchange doesn't just elevate the quality of the session; it makes participants feel seen and valued, which is a potent ingredient in fostering loyalty.

Don't let promotion slip through the cracks. In the days leading up to your live session, create buzz around it. Use your social media platforms to tease content, share countdowns, and hint at any special guests or surprises you might have in store. This promotional push not only boosts live attendance but also reels in viewers who might be new to your channel.

Speaking of visibility, collaboration can be a game-changer. Invite guests to your live sessions—industry experts, fellow influencers, or notable figures within your niche. This not only enriches your content but also exposes you to your guest's audience, widening your reach and potentially boosting your follower count.

Technical quality can't be overlooked. Ensure your audio and video quality are up to snuff. Poor sound or a glitchy feed can be a major turnoff and might discourage viewers from sticking around. Do a test run before going live to troubleshoot any potential issues.

Don't let the conversation end when your live session does. Follow up with a post-session recap on your platforms, encouraging further engagement. Share highlights or key takeaways and invite feedback for future sessions. This keeps the energy high and the conversation flowing, even after the live broadcast concludes.

Analyze and adapt. Make use of available analytics tools to gauge the success of your live sessions. Look at viewer numbers, engagement rates, and feedback to understand what's resonating with your audience. Use these insights to tweak and enhance future broadcasts.

Last but not least, don't be too hard on yourself. The beauty of live sessions lies in their authenticity and spontaneity. Each broadcast is a learning experience, so embrace the unexpected. Even seasoned pros encounter hiccups. What matters most is how you handle them—with grace, a sense of humor, and an unwavering commitment to your audience.

Live sessions are a powerful way to breathe life into your social media strategy. They offer a unique opportunity to interact directly with your audience, build community, and showcase the unfiltered, real you. Remember, growth on social media is not just about the numbers. It's about making meaningful connections, and live broadcasts are an excellent tool to do just that. So go live, share generously, engage sincerely, and watch your social media presence flourish.

Chapter 7:
Monetization Strategies

As we shift focus from nurturing your social media platforms to capitalizing on their potential, it's critical to dive into the sophisticated realm of monetization. Turning your social media presence into a source of income isn't just about hitting certain follower milestones; it's about engaging your audience in a way that's both genuine and strategic. Whether it's through partnering with brands that resonate with your values or selling your own merchandise or services directly to your followers, the opportunity to monetize hinges on the quality of your connections. This chapter outlines how to identify the right monetization strategies that align with your personal brand and audience expectations. Beyond direct sales and partnerships, we'll explore the basics of social media advertising, highlighting how to craft effective ad campaigns that amplify your earning potential without alienating your audience. Mastering budgeting and calculating return on investment (ROI) will empower you to make informed decisions that sustain and grow your social media empire financially. By embracing these monetization strategies, you're not just converting likes and follows into dollars; you're building a diversified portfolio of income streams that can withstand the test of time and algorithm changes.

Monetizing Your Social Media Presence

By now, you've laid the foundation for your social media empire, mastered the art of content creation, unlocked the secrets of going viral, and cultivated a genuinely engaged online community. The next logical step? Turning all that hard work into a steady income stream. Let's dive into the world of monetizing your social media presence, ensuring every like, share, and comment starts paying off in more tangible ways than just online clout.

The first thing you need to understand about monetization is that it's more than just making money. It's about creating value, both for yourself and your audience. This value exchange is at the heart of successful monetization strategies. It's not just about selling; it's about enhancing your relationship with your followers by providing them with offers that are relevant, helpful, and aligned with the content they've come to love from you.

A prime strategy for monetization is affiliate marketing. This involves promoting products or services to your audience and earning a commission for every sale made through your referral. The key here is authenticity. Choose to partner with brands that reflect your values and interests, and which you believe will genuinely benefit your followers. This maintains trust and credibility with your audience while opening up a revenue stream.

Another powerful avenue is sponsored content. Brands are constantly looking for influencers and content creators with engaged audiences to promote their products. However, transparency is critical. Always disclose sponsorship deals to your followers to maintain trust. Remember, the more niche and engaged your audience, the more valuable it is to advertisers, even if it isn't massive.

Creating and selling your own merchandise or digital products is also a fantastic way to monetize your social media presence. Whether it's e-books, courses, merch, or printables, leveraging your personal brand to sell products directly to your audience can turn your social media platforms into significant income sources. This method requires more upfront investment but can yield high returns and deepen your brand's relationship with your audience.

Subscription services and membership sites have gained traction as a monetization method. Platforms like Patreon allow creators to offer exclusive content, behind-the-scenes access, or special perks for a monthly subscription fee. This model rewards your most loyal followers with premium content while providing you with a predictable income stream.

Don't overlook the potential of hosting live events or workshops, either virtually or in person. These can be excellent opportunities to monetize your expertise and engage with your audience on a deeper level. Workshops, seminars, and webinars can all be ticketed or require a registration fee, adding another layer to your monetization strategy.

Partnerships and collaborations can also lead to monetization opportunities beyond the obvious sponsored content. Collaborating with other creators or brands to co-produce content or events can open up additional revenue streams through shared audiences and resources.

Advertising revenue should not be ignored, especially if you're active on platforms like YouTube. Once you meet their eligibility criteria, you can start earning money directly from the ads shown on your videos. This requires a significant amount of views to be substantial, but it's a passive income source once it's set up.

Consider offering consultation services as well. If you've successfully built a strong social media presence, there's a good chance you have valuable insights and skills that businesses and individuals are willing to pay for. Consulting can be a highly lucrative way to leverage your expertise.

Crowdfunding for specific projects or causes can also be a form of monetization. Platforms like Kickstarter allow you to gather financial support from your audience for particular initiatives, helping you bring new ideas to life while ensuring your followers feel directly involved in your success.

While incorporating these monetization strategies, it's crucial to continue delivering high-quality content and engaging with your audience. Monetization should feel like a natural extension of what you're already doing, not a departure from your brand's essence or an interruption to your content flow.

Remember, monetization success doesn't happen overnight. It requires patience, experimentation, and a deep understanding of what your audience values. Listen to their feedback, adjust your strategies accordingly, and treat monetization as an ongoing process rather than a one-time setup.

Finally, as you start earning from your social media presence, be mindful of the legal and financial implications. Understand the tax obligations and legal considerations around your income streams to ensure your monetization efforts don't just lead to success but are sustainable and compliant in the long term.

The journey to monetizing your social media presence is both exciting and challenging. With the right strategies, a focus on value, and a commitment to integrity and transparency, you can turn your followers into a flourishing income that rewards your hard work and creativity. The world of social media offers endless opportunities for those ready to seize them. Let your presence not just be influential but also financially rewarding.

Partnering with Brands As we dive deeper into the monetization strategies for your social media empire, a pivotal and often lucrative avenue is the partnership with brands. Mastering this facet of monetization not only boosts your income but also elevates your credibility and reach on the social media platforms. In this segment, we'll navigate through the nuances of forming, maintaining, and thriving through brand partnerships.

Initially, the concept of partnering with a brand might seem daunting. You may wonder, "Is my follower count high enough?" or "Do I fit the criteria that brands are looking for?" The answer isn't solely in the numbers. Instead, it's about engagement rate, the quality of content, and how your audience aligns with the brand's target market. Understanding your unique value proposition is your first step; knowing what you can offer to a brand that nobody else can is key to standing out.

Research is paramount. Not every brand is a perfect fit for your platform, and authenticity is crucial for a successful partnership. Endorse products or services that you genuinely like or use, as your audience can easily detect insincerity, which can harm your relationship with them. Compile a list of brands that align with your niche and values, and begin to understand their marketing goals and how you might help achieve them.

Crafting your pitch is the next crucial step. Your pitch to a brand should succinctly outline who you are, what you do, and how a partnership can benefit them. Include engagement metrics, demographic information of your audience, and examples of content that showcase your appeal and influence. Tailor each pitch to the specific brand, showing them that you've done your homework and understand their needs.

While reaching out, remember that persistence pays. You might not hear back from every brand, or you may receive rejections. It's part of the process. Be persistent but respectful, and continue refining your pitch and approach based on feedback and outcomes.

Once you've secured a partnership, clear communication is essential. Discuss expectations, deliverables, timelines, and compensation openly. Ensuring both parties are on the same page helps in building a strong and lasting relationship.

Executing the campaign comes next. High-quality content that seamlessly incorporates the brand while still resonating with your audience is paramount. Authenticity should shine through every sponsored post or story, reinforcing trust with your followers.

After the campaign, it's crucial to evaluate its performance. Providing brands with detailed reports on reach, engagement, and other relevant metrics showcases your professionalism and can open doors for future collaborations. This step is also an opportunity for self-assessment and learning, allowing you to refine your approach for the next partnership.

Moreover, it's vital to maintain a balance between sponsored and non-sponsored content. Too many promotions can alienate your audience, so it's crucial to keep providing value through your regular content. Engage with your audience about their thoughts on promotions and take their feedback into account for future endeavors.

Having a legal understanding is also important. Familiarize yourself with the FTC (Federal Trade Commission) guidelines on endorsements and advertising. Transparency with your audience about sponsored content is not only a legal requirement but also builds trust.

As your platform grows, so will your negotiations with brands. Learning negotiation skills can help you secure not only higher compensation but also deals that are more aligned with your brand and values. Understand your worth and don't be afraid to negotiate terms that reflect that.

Exploring long-term partnerships rather than one-off deals can provide stability and foster stronger connections with brands. These relationships can evolve into ambassadorships, where you become a face of the brand, which can significantly boost your credibility and influence.

Innovating within partnerships keeps your content fresh and engaging. Experiment with different content formats and strategies to keep your audience interested and attract new followers. This also demonstrates to brands your creativity and versatility.

Remember, the goal isn't just to make money but to build relationships - with both brands and your audience. Every partnership should feel like a natural extension of your online persona. Striking the right balance between authenticity and commercialism can be challenging, but it's the key to long-term success in partnering with brands.

Lastly, always be learning and evolving. The social media landscape and brand marketing strategies are constantly changing. Staying informed, adaptable, and proactive in seeking out new opportunities will ensure you remain a valuable partner to brands and an influential figure to your audience.

Securing and successfully executing brand partnerships is a testament to your influence and hard work in building your social media presence. It's a significant stepping stone in monetizing and scaling your empire, so approach each opportunity with diligence, creativity, and integrity.

Selling Merchandise or Services seamlessly weaves into the fabric of a successful social media strategy. It's not just about broadcasting your offerings; it's about fitting them into the narrative you're building online. When it comes to monetizing your social media influence, selling directly to your audience can be a game-changer, turning followers into customers, and customers into evangelists for your brand.

First things first, understanding what your audience needs and values is paramount. You've spent time drawing them in with engaging content and building trust through consistent, authentic interactions. This foundation is critical because when you start selling, you aren't seen as just another advertiser; you're a trusted figure recommending a product or service that can add value to their lives.

Once you've honed in on what your audience might be interested in buying, the next step is to consider the logistics. Whether it's merchandise related to your brand or services that you offer, seamless integration into your content is key. This could mean showcasing your products in use through stories or posts, offering behind-the-scenes looks at your services, or even conducting live demonstrations to engage your audience and show the real value of what you're selling.

When it comes to setting up the sale, several e-commerce platforms are specifically designed to integrate with social media. Leveraging these tools can simplify the process for both you and your customers, making it as easy as a few clicks to go from seeing a product in your post to completing a purchase. Highlighting ease of purchase, with clear calls to action, can significantly improve conversion rates.

Pricing strategy also plays a crucial role in selling through social media. It's essential to strike a balance between what your audience is willing to pay and the value that your product or service provides. Offering exclusive discounts or promotions to your social media followers can also incentivize purchases, making your audience feel like they are part of an exclusive club.

Feedback and engagement shouldn't stop after a sale. Encouraging customers to share their experiences with your products or services on social media not only provides you with valuable testimonials but also engages your community. It transforms customers into active participants in your brand story, further blurring the lines between seller and buyer, influencer and influenced.

Another key factor to consider is customer service. Social media platforms offer a unique opportunity to offer quick and personal customer service. Addressing concerns, answering questions, and offering support through these platforms can enhance your brand's reputation and lead to higher customer satisfaction and loyalty.

Keep in mind, the goal isn't just to make a sale but to build a relationship. This means listening to your audience, responding to their needs, and continuously adapting your offerings. It's a dynamic process that, when done right, can significantly augment your social media strategy and help you monetize your presence in a meaningful way.

In terms of content integration, storytelling is a powerful tool. Crafting narratives around your products or services that resonate with your audience can make your offerings more than just items for purchase; they become part of a lifestyle or set of values that your brand represents. This connection can deeply influence buying behavior, turning your merchandise or services into symbols of a larger community or cause.

Additionally, leveraging user-generated content is a powerful strategy. Encouraging your followers to share their own experiences with your products or services not only provides you with authentic content to repost but also builds a community around your brand. This strategy helps in two ways: it validates your offerings through real-life testimonials and deepens your relationship with your community by showcasing their contributions.

Analysis and adaptation are crucial throughout this process. Monitoring sales data, social media engagement metrics, and customer feedback will provide insights into what's working and what isn't. This information is invaluable for refining your approach, whether it's tweaking your content strategy, adjusting your pricing, or even rethinking the products or services you offer.

Don't forget the power of exclusivity. Limited-time offers, exclusive products, or services for your social media followers can create a sense of urgency and exclusivity that motivates purchases. This strategy can be particularly effective during product launches or special promotions, helping to drive engagement and sales.

Finally, collaboration can amplify your efforts. Partnering with influencers or other brands that share your values and audience can expand your reach and lend credibility to your offerings. These partnerships can take various forms, from joint giveaways to collaborative products or services, each adding value to your brand in the eyes of your audience.

In conclusion, selling merchandise or services through social media is about much more than the transaction. It's about continuing to engage your audience, providing them with value, and building relationships that go beyond the buyer-seller dynamic. With the right strategy, your social media platform can not only boost your sales but also strengthen your brand and deepen your connection with your community.

The journey from content creator to e-commerce success story is filled with opportunities for growth, both personally and professionally. It requires a nuanced understanding of your audience, a strategic approach to content, and a commitment to providing value at every turn. Yet, for those willing to put in the effort, the rewards can be substantial, transforming your social media presence into a thriving, revenue-generating ecosystem.

Introduction to Social Media Advertising

Transitioning into the realm of monetization, it's impossible to overlook the dynamic role of social media advertising. At its core, social media adverts are about harnessing the immense reach of platforms to not just display your message, but to ensure it resonates with the right audience, at the right time. Imagine distilling the essence of your brand or content into a captivating narrative, then leveraging the sophisticated targeting tools provided by platforms to put this narrative in front of individuals who are most likely to engage with it, and ultimately, convert. This precision targeting isn't just about boosting your visibility or follower count; it's about smartly investing resources to achieve measurable returns. Whether you're a budding influencer eager to land your first brand partnership, or an entrepreneur ready to sky-rocket your product sales, understanding how to navigate the complexities of social media ads is pivotal. It's about finding that sweet spot between creativity and analytics, where compelling content meets strategic placement to not only amplify your reach but to also solidify your monetization potential.

Running Effective Ad Campaigns If you're aiming to make a splash on social media, mastering the art of advertising is crucial. It's more than just throwing money at ads and hoping for the best. It's about precision, strategy, and understanding the complexities of different platforms. Let's dive into how you can run ad campaigns that don't just reach people but resonate with them, turning viewers into followers, and followers into fans.

First things first, your campaign needs a clear goal. Are you looking to increase brand awareness, drive traffic to your website, or maybe boost sales for a product launch? Pinpointing your objective will shape the entirety of your campaign, from the ad content to the targeted audience. It helps to keep your goals SMART: Specific, Measurable, Achievable, Relevant, and Time-bound. A well-defined goal is your north star, guiding every decision you make.

Understanding your audience is non-negotiable. Who are they? What do they like? How do they consume content? The answers to these questions are golden. They help you tailor your ads to speak directly to your audience's interests and pain points. Remember, a generic message fails to cut through the noise. Use social media analytics and tools to dig deeper into demographics, interests, and behavior patterns. The more you know your audience, the more targeted and effective your ads will be.

Now, let's talk platforms. Each social media platform has its vibe, its language, and its unique way of engaging users. An ad that performs well on Instagram might not have the same impact on Facebook or TikTok. It's essential to adapt your campaign to fit the platform it's running on. This means understanding the platform's algorithms, the preferred type of content, and even the optimal times to post. Customization is key.

Creativity in your ads can't be overstated. In a sea of content, your ads need to stand out. This is where eye-catching visuals, compelling copy, and strong calls to action come into play. But creativity also means thinking outside the box with your ad formats. Don't just stick to image or video ads; explore carousel ads, story ads, or even interactive polls to engage your audience differently.

Creating a seamless user journey is crucial for conversion. Your ad caught their eye, great, but what happens next? Ensure that the landing page or the call to action aligns with the ad's message. A disjointed journey from ad to action can cause friction and result in lost opportunities. Simplicity and clarity in what you want your audience to do after they see your ad can significantly boost your conversion rates.

Budgeting wisely ensures that your ad spend is an investment, not just an expense. Start with a test budget to see which ads perform best, then allocate more funds to the high performers. Use platform tools to optimize your ad spend for the best outcomes, whether that's more engagement, leads, or sales. Remember, throwing more money at an underperforming ad won't magically fix it. Analyze, adjust, and act.

Measurement and analysis are where the magic happens. By setting up proper tracking, you can see which ads drive action and which fall flat. Dive deep into the data to understand why. Maybe it's the messaging, the targeting, or even the timing. Use these insights to iterate and improve your future campaigns. Remember, every campaign, successful or not, provides valuable lessons.

Lastly, stay up to date with the latest trends and features on social media platforms. Social media is ever-evolving, and so are its advertising opportunities. New ad formats, targeting options, and analytics tools are constantly being rolled out. Staying informed allows you to adapt your strategies, experiment with new features, and always stay one step ahead.

Running effective ad campaigns on social media requires a mix of strategic planning, creative thinking, and rigorous analysis. By setting clear goals, knowing your audience, adapting to each platform, creating standout ads, and continually optimizing based on data, you can run campaigns that not only reach but resonate with your target audience. It's a powerful way to grow your online presence, engage with your community, and achieve your business objectives on social media.

Budgeting and ROI Transitioning into the world of social media advertising requires a keen understanding of both budgeting and return on investment (ROI). It's not just about throwing money at your campaigns and hoping for the best. Instead, it's about smart investments, tracking progress, and continuously optimizing your strategy to ensure the best possible outcomes. When you start to pour funds into social media advertising, it's crucial to set a budget that aligns with your goals but doesn't break the bank. This delicate balance is where your journey begins.

First off, let's talk about setting your budget. It's tempting to believe that significant investment equals significant returns. However, the truth of the matter is that prudence and strategy often outperform sheer financial might. Start small, testing different ad formats and platforms to see which ones connect best with your target audience. This experimental phase is essential and should be factored into your initial budget. Keep in mind, the goal here isn't immediate profit, but rather, gathering valuable data that will inform your larger strategy moving forward.

Now, onto ROI, which is the meat of any advertising strategy. Calculating your ROI involves tracking not just the obvious metrics like clicks and impressions, but also how these translate into tangible outcomes for your business. Are viewers converting by making purchases, signing up for newsletters, or downloading your app? Each of these actions has value, and understanding this value is key to evaluating the effectiveness of your campaigns. Remember, a high ROI means that your advertising efforts are not just bringing in views, but driving meaningful engagement that contributes to your bottom line.

Adjustment and optimization are the next steps in your journey. With a clear picture of what's working and what's not, you can begin reallocating your budget to the most effective channels and ad formats. This is where your initial experimentation pays off. You're no longer shooting in the dark but making informed decisions that amplify your success. It's a constant cycle of testing, learning, and optimizing. Remember, the social media landscape is ever-evolving, and flexibility is your best weapon in staying ahead.

In conclusion, mastering budgeting and ROI in social media advertising is not just about the money you spend, but how wisely you spend it. It's about setting realistic budgets, understanding the value of different actions within your funnel, and constantly refining your approach to ensure that every dollar spent is an investment in your future success. As you move forward, keep this mindful approach at the forefront of your strategy. It's not just about growing your social media empire; it's about doing so in a way that is sustainable, effective, and ultimately profitable.

Chapter 8:
Scaling Your Empire

Now that we've laid the groundwork for monetizing your social media and teased out how engagement and virality can amplify your presence, let's dive into the mechanics of scaling your empire. The shift from a solo operation to a burgeoning empire isn't just about working harder; it's about working smarter. Building a dedicated team can transform your efforts, allowing you to delegate tasks that eat into your creative time. This doesn't mean losing control; it's about empowering others to help carry your vision forward. Equally crucial is automating and streamlining your processes. With the right tools and systems in place, you're freed up to focus on big-picture strategies rather than getting bogged down by the day-to-day operations.

Diversifying your income streams also plays a pivotal role in scaling. Relying solely on ad revenue or partnerships can be risky. Exploring various monetization channels – be it through digital products, exclusive memberships, or even educational workshops – can provide stability and ensure your empire isn't vulnerable to shifts in social media algorithms or market trends. As your digital footprint grows, staying agile will be your most powerful asset. By embracing these pillars of scaling, you're not just expanding your reach; you're building a resilient and dynamic social media empire capable of weathering the storms and seizing the opportunities that lie ahead in an ever-evolving landscape.

Building a Team

When you're scaling your social media empire, an essential step is building a solid team. This might seem like a luxury at first, but as your presence and ambitions grow, it becomes a necessity. A team can provide you with the support you need to focus on the bigger picture while ensuring the day-to-day tasks are handled efficiently.

First, let's talk about identifying the roles you need. The core roles might include content creators, graphic designers, videographers, a social media manager, and analytics experts. Each of these roles plays a crucial part in maintaining the quality of your content, engaging with your audience, and analyzing the effectiveness of your strategies.

Hiring the right people is more than just finding individuals with the right skills; it's about finding people who share your vision and passion. They should be as committed to growing your social media empire as you are. Conduct interviews that not only assess their technical capabilities and experience but also explore their motivation and cultural fit.

Once your team is in place, effective communication becomes the backbone of your operation. Establish clear channels of communication, whether through regular meetings, a project management tool, or a group chat. Everyone should feel comfortable sharing their ideas, concerns, and feedback.

Delegating tasks is another critical aspect of team management. It might be challenging to let go of certain tasks, especially if you've been handling everything yourself. However, delegation is key to scaling your business. Trust your team's capabilities and give them the autonomy they need to succeed.

Collaboration within your team can lead to innovative ideas and strategies, but it requires fostering a creative and open environment. Encourage team members to collaborate and brainstorm together.

Sometimes, the best ideas come from casual conversations or team meetings.

Setting goals and expectations is crucial for tracking progress and ensuring everyone is aligned. These goals should be realistic, measurable, and time-bound. Celebrate successes together as a team, and learn from failures without assigning blame.

Investing in your team's growth is an investment in your empire's future. Provide opportunities for learning and professional development. Attend conferences together, provide access to online courses, or bring in experts for workshops.

As your empire grows, your team's structure might need to adapt. Be open to restructuring roles and responsibilities to better suit your evolving needs. This flexibility allows you to leverage your team's strengths effectively.

Don't underestimate the importance of team culture. A positive, supportive culture can boost morale and productivity. Organize team-building activities, whether virtual or in-person, to strengthen relationships within your team.

Feedback loops are essential for continuous improvement. Implement a system for providing and receiving feedback, both positive and constructive. This should apply to you as well; be open to feedback from your team on how you can better support them.

Handling conflicts professionally and promptly is vital. Misunderstandings and disagreements are natural, but they shouldn't fester. Address issues head-on, with a focus on resolution and learning.

Lastly, celebrate your team. Recognize individual and collective achievements. This not only boosts morale but also reinforces their value to your empire. A simple thank you, public recognition, or reward can go a long way.

In summary, building and managing a team is a significant step in scaling your social media empire. It requires careful planning, open communication, and a strong culture of collaboration and feedback. With the right team in place, you can focus on strategic growth, knowing the day-to-day operations are in capable hands. Your team will be the driving force behind your success, so invest in them, support them, and grow together.

Remember, your empire wasn't built in a day, and it wasn't built alone. With the right team by your side, the possibilities are endless. Embrace the journey, and see just how far you can go together.

Automating and Streamlining Your Processes

As you venture into the journey of scaling your empire, it's imperative to recognize the importance of efficiency. With your social media presence growing and your engagements skyrocketing, managing everything manually isn't just impractical; it's nearly impossible. That's where automating and streamlining your processes come into play, acting as the backbone of your expanding empire.

First off, let's talk automation tools. There's a plethora of options out there designed to take the grunt work off your hands. From scheduling posts across platforms to automated responses to common queries, these tools not only save time but also ensure that your online presence is consistent and ever-engaging. It allows you to focus more on creating content and strategizing rather than getting bogged down by the nitty-gritty of posting schedules.

Streamlining isn't just about automation, though. It's also about refining your processes to make them more efficient. This might mean creating templates for your posts or developing a content calendar that aligns with your strategic goals. By having standardized processes in place, you're able to maintain a high level of quality across your posts, ensuring that your message is clear, cohesive, and compelling.

A key component in streamlining is leveraging analytics. By understanding which posts perform well, you're in a better position to tailor your content strategy accordingly, focusing on what resonates with your audience. Analytics tools can automate much of this analysis, identifying trends and insights that might not be immediately obvious.

Another aspect to consider is the delegation of tasks. As you scale, building a team becomes essential. However, managing a team presents its own set of challenges. Using project management and collaboration tools can streamline communication, keeping everyone on the same page and ensuring tasks are completed on time.

Email marketing, although not new, is a critical component of maintaining engagement off-platform. Automating email campaigns allows for consistent communication with your followers, providing them with value outside of social media. Plus, it's an excellent avenue for personalization, which can significantly boost your engagement rates.

Don't forget about the content creation process. Automating aspects of content creation, such as graphic design or video editing, through the use of software and templates can drastically reduce the time spent on these tasks. This means more time for brainstorming and strategy planning.

When embarking on automation, it's crucial to maintain a balance. Over-automation can lead to a loss of personal touch, so it's important to identify areas where human intervention is necessary, like community engagement or content ideation.

Investing in the right tools is paramount. While it might be tempting to go for cheaper or free options, remember that these are the tools upon which your empire is being built and scaled. Opt for solutions that offer the right mix of features, reliability, and scalability.

Furthermore, as you streamline and automate, staying up to date with the latest trends and technologies is key. The digital landscape is continually evolving, and what works today might not work tomorrow. Keeping abreast of these changes ensures that your processes remain efficient and effective.

Security should never be overlooked. Automating and streamlining processes involve handling vast amounts of data, including sensitive information. Ensure that whatever tools or practices you integrate into your strategy prioritize data protection and adhere to privacy regulations.

It's also beneficial to create a feedback loop within your processes. Regularly review the efficiency and effectiveness of your automation and streamlining efforts. This can involve analytics, but also direct feedback from your audience and team. Use this feedback to make continuous improvements.

Lastly, don't underestimate the power of experimentation. The fear of failure can often be a hindrance to trying out new tools or processes. However, experimentation is crucial for innovation and can lead to significant improvements in how you manage your social media empire.

To wrap up, automating and streamlining your processes is not just about making things easier for yourself; it's about creating a sustainable foundation upon which your social media empire can thrive. Taking the time to implement these strategies will pay dividends in the long run, allowing you to focus on what truly matters—engaging your audience, creating compelling content, and achieving your strategic goals.

Remember, as your empire grows, so too should your methods evolve. Stay flexible, be willing to adapt, and always keep your ultimate goal in sight: to grow, monetize, and make a lasting impact on the digital landscape.

Diversifying Your Income Streams

Now that we've covered the essentials of building, growing, and beginning to monetize your social media empire, let's pivot to a strategy crucial for long-term success: diversifying your income streams. In the vast world of social media, relying on a single source of income can be akin to walking a tightrope without a safety net. The digital landscape is ever-changing - platforms evolve, trends come and go, and what worked yesterday might not work tomorrow. Hence, diversifying is not just a strategy; it's a necessity.

First off, understand that diversification means more than having multiple social media accounts across various platforms. While that's a good start, true diversification involves tapping into different revenue streams that can operate independently. This means if one stream dries up, you're not left high and dry.

Let's start with an extension of what many of you might already be doing: partnering with brands. Yes, brand partnerships are a great income stream, but have you considered leveraging these partnerships beyond one-off posts? Think in terms of long-term relationships, exclusive deals, or even becoming a brand ambassador. These arrangements often come with more substantial financial perks and can provide a steady income over time.

Another avenue ripe for exploration is creating and selling your merchandise. This approach not only diversifies your income but also strengthens your personal brand. Merchandise can range from t-shirts and hats to digital products like ebooks or courses. The key is to make sure whatever you're selling resonates with your audience and adds value to their lives.

Don't underestimate the power of leveraging your knowledge through paid workshops, webinars, or online courses. If you've mastered the art of social media, why not teach others and get paid for it? This can be particularly lucrative as you're essentially monetizing the skills and knowledge you've already acquired. Plus, online education is a booming market, with people constantly looking to learn and improve their skills.

Consider diving into the world of affiliate marketing. By promoting others' products and earning a commission for sales made through your referral, you're tapping into a virtually limitless market. The beauty of affiliate marketing is its scalability and the fact that it can be integrated seamlessly into your existing content.

Then there's the realm of digital content creation. Beyond the usual suspects of photos and videos, think ebooks, guides, or premium content behind a subscription model. This not only diversifies your income but also deepens your relationship with your most dedicated followers who are willing to pay for that extra value you're providing.

Ad revenue can also be a significant income stream, especially if you're active on platforms like YouTube. As your viewership grows, so does your potential to earn through ads. But remember, ad revenue can be unpredictable, further underscoring the need for multiple income streams.

While exploring new income avenues, don't ignore the potential of in-person events. Hosting workshops, meet-ups, or speaking at conferences can open up new revenue streams and expand your network. In a digital world, the power of physical presence and human connection can be surprisingly lucrative.

Social media consulting is another path worth considering. Many businesses are looking to expand their digital footprint but don't know how. With your expertise, you can guide them to success and charge a premium for your services.

Investing in related business ventures can be a more advanced, yet rewarding strategy. Use the income you've generated from your social media platforms to invest in startups, apps, or other businesses that align with your brand. It's a way to let your money work for you, potentially opening up entirely new income streams.

Remember, the goal of diversifying isn't just to earn more money—it's to build a more resilient business. The digital world is fraught with uncertainty; algorithms change, platforms rise and fall, and audience tastes evolve. By having multiple income streams, you can weather the storms and ensure the longevity of your empire.

When embarking on this journey of diversification, it's crucial to stay true to your brand and audience. Every new venture or revenue stream should feel like a natural extension of what you already do. If it feels forced or off-brand, your audience will notice, and it could harm your brand integrity.

Also, it's essential to maintain a balance. Diversification doesn't mean spreading yourself so thin that the quality of your content or your engagement with your audience suffers. It's about finding the right mix of income streams that allow you to grow sustainably while still delivering the value your audience expects.

In conclusion, diversifying your income streams is not an optional strategy for scaling your social media empire—it's an imperative. As you navigate this journey, stay flexible, adaptable, and always be on the lookout for new opportunities. The digital world moves fast, but with a diversified approach, you'll not only keep up but thrive.

Remember, the path to diversification is a marathon, not a sprint. It takes time, effort, and sometimes, a bit of trial and error to find what works best for you and your brand. But with perseverance and a strategic approach, you can build a robust, diversified income portfolio that will sustain your social media empire for years to come.

Chapter 9:
Navigating Challenges

As we float further into the mechanics of building a dynamic social media presence, it's pivotal to address the bumps and storms you're bound to face. Challenges such as dealing with negative feedback, overcoming growth plateaus, and staying afloat in the constantly evolving social media landscape are part and parcel of the journey. When the inevitable wave of critiques crashes in, it's crucial to harness it constructively—feedback, both good and bad, can be a goldmine for growth when approached with the right mindset. Similarly, hitting a growth plateau isn't a stop signal but a nudge to reassess and recalibrate your strategies. Possibly, it's time to inject fresh content ideas, pivot your approach, or even engage with your audience on a new level. Meanwhile, the social media sands are always shifting; what works today might not tomorrow. Staying relevant demands a blend of sticking to your core while also being agile enough to evolve with trends and algorithm changes. It's not just about riding the wave but also being ready to adapt your sails to continue making headway in this vast, virtual ocean. Remember, navigating through these challenges isn't just about survival—it's about learning, growing, and thriving in the ever-competitive realm of social media.

Dealing with Negative Feedback

When you're building a social media empire, you're going to face your fair share of challenges, and one of the most daunting can be handling negative feedback. It's an inevitable part of the digital landscape.

Whether it's a less-than-flattering comment on your latest post or a direct message expressing dissatisfaction, how you respond can significantly impact your brand.

First and foremost, it's crucial to approach negative feedback with a level head. Reacting impulsively or defensively can often exacerbate the situation. Instead, take a deep breath and try to see the critique from the commenter's perspective. This approach can help you respond more empathetically and constructively.

Not all feedback needs a public response. In some cases, addressing the concern privately can prevent the situation from escalating. A direct message offering to solve the problem or simply apologizing can go a long way in turning a critic into a supporter.

However, when responding publicly, remember: the internet has a long memory. Crafting a thoughtful, respectful response can not only resolve the immediate issue but also demonstrate to others that you're committed to customer satisfaction. It shows you're not just interested in the spotlight but are also attentive to your audience's needs and opinions.

It's also vital to distinguish between constructive criticism and outright trolling. Constructive feedback, even when negative, can provide valuable insights into areas where you can improve. Treating these opportunities with appreciation can fuel your growth and refinement. On the other hand, trolls seek to provoke and should often be ignored or, if necessary, blocked.

Embracing negative feedback as a growth opportunity is a mindset shift that can transform your social media presence. Every critique gives you the chance to fine-tune your content, improve your engagement strategies, and better align with your audience's expectations. This proactive stance can turn potential setbacks into steps forward.

Creating a feedback loop where your followers feel heard and valued is another pivotal strategy. Encourage open dialogue by asking for opinions and showing that you're acting on the feedback received. This approach not only improves your content and strategies but also strengthens your community.

Maintaining a sense of humor can also be a valuable asset when dealing with negative feedback. A witty, light-hearted response to a less-than-kind comment can often defuse tension and endear you further to your audience. Remember, the goal is to build relationships, not just a follower count.

Invest in community management as your platform grows. Having a team or a dedicated individual to monitor comments and feedback can help you stay on top of the conversation. They can flag issues that need your attention and ensure that the community remains a positive space for everyone.

Document your experiences with feedback, both positive and negative. Keeping a record can help you identify patterns or recurring issues that need addressing. This practice can inform your content strategy, helping you to create more resonant and engaging posts.

Offering an olive branch can sometimes turn a negative interaction into a positive outcome. Whether it's offering a discount, a free product, or simply a more in-depth conversation to resolve the issue, showing that you're willing to go above and beyond can often win back disgruntled followers.

Remember, not all feedback will be fair or reasonable. It's important to know your own value and not compromise your vision based on every piece of criticism. Finding the balance between being responsive and staying true to your brand is key.

Stay consistent in your responses. Whether it's a positive or negative comment, showing that you consistently engage with your audience can foster a more inclusive and welcoming community. This consistency can also set expectations for how interactions on your platform are handled.

Finally, learn to let go when necessary. While engaging with feedback is crucial, dwelling on every negative comment is not healthy or productive. Focus on constructive criticism and move forward with your goals, using the feedback to fuel your journey, not hinder it.

In the world of social media, dealing with negative feedback is an art form in itself. It requires patience, empathy, and a strategic approach. By embracing criticism as an opportunity for growth, maintaining a respectful and positive attitude, and knowing when to engage or disengage, you can navigate the choppy waters of online feedback and emerge stronger, wiser, and more connected to your audience than ever before.

Overcoming Plateaus in Growth

Reaching a plateau in your social media growth can feel like hitting an invisible wall. It's a common challenge, but not insurmountable. The key lies in identifying the root causes and implementing strategies that push you beyond the current limits. This endeavor requires a blend of creativity, analysis, and sometimes, a willingness to overhaul your existing approach.

Firstly, it's crucial to conduct a thorough audit of your content. This means looking beyond surface-level engagement metrics to understand the deeper impact of your posts. Are you truly engaging your audience, or just catching their fleeting attention? The difference is significant. Engaging content prompts interaction, shares, and discussions, creating a vibrant community around your brand or persona. If your content lacks this depth, it's time to innovate.

Revisiting your target audience analysis is also essential. Over time, audiences can evolve, developing new interests or moving away from platforms altogether. If you're not continuously refining your understanding of your audience, you risk becoming irrelevant. Surveys, direct engagement, and social listening tools can provide fresh insights into what your audience cares about now.

Another strategy is to diversify your content types. If you've primarily focused on images, consider how videos, live streams, or even interactive content could add variety. Each content type has unique benefits and can attract different segments of your audience. Experimentation is vital; without it, you'll never discover new growth avenues.

Don't overlook the power of collaboration. Partnering with influencers or brands that share a mutual audience can introduce you to new followers. These partnerships should be more than mere shoutouts; aim for collaborations that add value to all parties involved, especially the audience.

Additionally, it's essential to stay abreast of platform changes and algorithm updates. What worked last year might not work today. Social media platforms are constantly tweaking their algorithms to improve user experience, which can have direct implications on your visibility. Regularly educating yourself about these changes and adapting your strategy accordingly is non-negotiable.

Investing in social media advertising can also help push past growth plateaus. Even a modest budget can significantly extend your reach if spent wisely. The key is to target your ads carefully, ensuring they're seen by those most likely to engage with your content genuinely.

Another critical area is SEO for social media. Yes, SEO isn't just for websites. Optimizing your profile and content for search can attract new followers looking for what you have to offer. Research relevant keywords and incorporate them into your bio, posts, and hashtags to improve your visibility in search results.

Speaking of hashtags, refining your hashtag strategy can also spur growth. Instead of using generic or overly broad hashtags, focus on those that are specific to your niche and content. This can help you reach a more targeted audience that's likely to be interested in your content.

Consistency in posting can't be ignored either. A common reason for hitting a growth plateau is irregular posting schedules, which can disengage your audience. Establishing and sticking to a consistent posting schedule keeps your audience engaged and can attract new followers.

Creating challenges or user-generated content campaigns can also reinvigorate your growth. These not only engage your current followers but, when shared, can attract attention from their networks as well. It's a powerful tool for organic growth, creating a sense of community and participation.

Don't neglect the power of data analysis. Use the analytics tools provided by social platforms to understand what's working and what isn't. This can provide valuable insights into the types of content that resonate most with your audience, the best times to post, and more. Leveraging this data can help you make informed decisions to break through your plateau.

Remember, overcoming a plateau requires patience and persistence. Growth strategies don't yield immediate results; they build over time. It's crucial to monitor your progress, adjust strategies as needed, and remain committed to your growth.

Finally, consider seeking feedback directly from your audience. Sometimes, the most straightforward approach to understanding what you could do differently is to ask. Use polls, question stickers on Instagram Stories, or direct messages to gather feedback. This not only provides you with actionable insights but also deepens your relationship with your followers.

In summary, breaking through a growth plateau on social media is challenging but entirely possible with the right strategies. It requires a deep understanding of your audience, a willingness to adapt and innovate, and a commitment to analyzing and optimizing your approach continuously. By diversifying your content, embracing collaboration, staying up-to-date with platform changes, and leveraging advertising and SEO, you can reignite your growth and continue building your social media empire.

Staying Relevant in an Ever-Changing Landscape

In the realm of social media, the ground is always shifting. What worked yesterday might not cut it today. So how do you keep your footing and continue to captivate your audience? Let's dive into essential strategies that promise to keep you ahead in this ever-changing landscape.

Firstly, it's crucial to stay informed. The digital world evolves at breakneck speed, and staying up-to-date with the latest trends and platform updates is non-negotiable. Make it a habit to check in with industry news sites and follow thought leaders who share insightful content. This proactive approach will arm you with the knowledge to pivot your strategies effectively.

Understanding your audience is your compass in the digital world. Keep a close ear to the ground and listen to their conversations, preferences, and feedback. Social media isn't just about broadcasting—it's a two-way dialogue. Engage with your followers, conduct polls, and ask questions to gauge their interests and adjust your content accordingly.

Embracing change is part of the game. Social media platforms are known for rolling out new features and algorithms that can make or break your visibility. Test new formats like short-form videos, Stories, or even new platforms altogether to see what resonates with your audience. Being an early adopter can give you a significant advantage.

Content versatility is your ally. While it's vital to have a niche, incorporating variety within your content can prevent your feed from becoming stale. Experiment with different types of content, such as tutorials, behind-the-scenes peeks, or even guest takeovers. This not only keeps your audience engaged but also broadens your appeal to potential followers.

Community building should be at the heart of your strategy. A dedicated community is a loyal one. Foster an environment where your followers feel valued and part of something bigger. Regularly recognizing and interacting with your community can turn casual followers into ardent supporters.

Leverage data to steer your course. Analytics aren't just numbers—they're insights into what's working and what's not. Delve into your performance metrics to understand which content types, posting times, and engagement strategies yield the best results. This data-driven approach will fine-tune your strategy for maximum impact.

Innovation is your best bet in staying relevant. Don't be afraid to try novel content ideas or storytelling techniques. Sometimes, it's the most unexpected content that breaks through the noise. Test different creative approaches, and remember, failure is just part of the learning process.

Collaboration can be a powerful tool for growth and relevance. Teaming up with other creators or brands can not only increase your exposure but also introduce fresh perspectives to your content. Look for synergies within your niche where a collaborative effort could be mutually beneficial.

Authenticity should never be compromised. In an age of polished feeds and curated personas, genuine connections stand out. Stay true to your voice and values, and don't chase trends that don't resonate with your brand. Authenticity fosters trust, and trust breeds loyalty.

Adapting your narrative to current events and social issues can increase relatability and relevance. However, it's important to approach sensitive topics with care and respect. Being socially aware and responsive can strengthen your relationship with your audience.

Mindset plays a pivotal role in navigating the digital landscape. Cultivate resilience and view challenges as opportunities to grow and innovate. The path to sustained relevance is fraught with setbacks, but a positive and adaptive mindset will keep you moving forward.

Don't shy away from feedback. Constructive criticism can be a goldmine of insights for improvement. Encourage your audience to share their thoughts on what they'd like to see more (or less) of. This direct feedback loop can guide your content development in a direction that resonates more deeply with your followers.

Finally, continuous learning is the foundation of staying relevant. The social media universe is vast, with endless possibilities to explore. Invest in courses, attend webinars, and read extensively. Broadening your knowledge and skills will empower you to craft compelling, fresh content that stands the test of time.

In conclusion, staying relevant in an ever-changing landscape requires a blend of strategies, from embracing new platforms and formats to fostering community and leveraging data. However, the core of these efforts lies in your ability to listen, adapt, and connect authentically with your audience. With these approaches, you're not just keeping up—you're setting the pace.

Remember, the only constant in social media is change itself. By staying agile, informed, and engaged, you'll navigate these waters with confidence and continue to grow your empire, one post at a time.

Chapter 10:
Case Studies of Successful Social Media Empires

Transitioning from the struggles highlighted in the previous chapter, it's time to shift gears and explore the sunnier side of social media—the empires that made it, against all odds. By examining the trajectories of influential **influencers**, iconic **brands**, and visionary **entrepreneurs**, this chapter aims to distill actionable insights and strategies that can help aspiring social media moguls carve out their own piece of the digital stratosphere. These case studies aren't just stories; they're a roadmap filled with practical nuggets on growing follower bases, engaging communities, and turning likes and shares into a lucrative business model. From an influencer who doubled their reach organically within a year, to a brand that mastered the art of viral marketing, and an entrepreneur whose innovative approach to content creation disrupted an entire industry, each case presents unique lessons on navigating social media's choppy waters. By understanding the decisions they made, the challenges they faced, and how they exploited the peculiarities of different platforms, readers will find inspiration and guidance on their journey to social media stardom.

Influencers

In the expansive world of social media, influencers have carved out empires that not only boast vast audiences but also demonstrate profound engagement and loyalty. This chapter delves into the strategic maneuvers and operational tactics employed by these social media titans. We'll explore how understanding the mechanics behind their success can provide invaluable insights for your journey to social media prominence.

At the heart of every influencer's success is their unwavering dedication to their niche. Thriving on authenticity, these individuals have mastered the art of turning personal passions into content that resonates. It's this heartfelt content that magnetizes audiences, turning casual viewers into devout followers. This suggests that the first step in scaling the heights of social media isn't to chase trends blindly but to find your unique voice within your niche.

Understanding the algorithm is akin to possessing the hidden map that guides you through the treacherous terrains of social media. Top influencers don't just post content; they strategically align it with the platform's algorithm, ensuring maximum visibility. Whether it's Instagram's preference for high-engagement posts or YouTube's love for longer watch times, knowing the rules of the game allows influencers to tailor their content for optimal performance.

Engagement is the lifeblood of any influencer's empire. Rather than viewing their followers as mere numbers, successful influencers engage with their audience in meaningful ways. This could be through responding to comments, hosting Q&A sessions, or sharing behind-the-scenes content. Such interactions not only boost engagement metrics but also build a community around the influencer's brand.

Cross-promotion and collaboration play a crucial role in an influencer's growth strategy. By partnering with peers within and outside their niche, influencers can tap into new audiences while providing fresh content to their followers. These collaborations often lead to a mutually beneficial growth spurt for all parties involved.

Another key factor in the meteoric rise of influencers is their ability to leverage trends. By staying abreast of current memes, challenges, and topics of interest, influencers can create content that's both relevant and relatable. This not only fuels immediate engagement but also positions the influencer as a go-to source for fresh and captivating content.

The savvy influencer knows the importance of diversifying income streams. Beyond brand deals and sponsored posts, successful influencers explore merchandise lines, digital products, and even exclusive content platforms. By not putting all their eggs in one basket, they ensure a steady income flow that's not overly reliant on the whims of algorithm changes or market trends.

Monetization is undoubtedly a significant goal for many social media influencers. However, the journey to successful monetization is paved with strategic brand partnerships that align with the influencer's brand identity. These collaborations must feel natural and authentic to the audience to maintain trust and engagement.

An influencer's toolkit is incomplete without a deep understanding of analytics. By regularly reviewing performance metrics, influencers can discern what works and what doesn't. This constant cycle of analysis and adjustment is what allows them to remain at the peak of their performance, ensuring that their content consistently resonates with their audience.

Despite the glamour and success, the path of an influencer is fraught with challenges such as audience saturation and burnout. Navigating these obstacles requires resilience, flexibility, and a willingness to innovate. The most successful influencers view challenges as opportunities to evolve, constantly finding new ways to captivate their audience.

One cannot overlook the role of storytelling in an influencer's success. The ability to weave personal experiences, insights, and lessons into a compelling narrative is what sets apart engaging content from the mundane. It fosters a deeper connection with the audience, making the influencer's journey an integral part of the audience's digital experience.

Maintaining authenticity in the face of commercial success is a fine line that influencers must tread. The audience's trust is hard-earned but easily lost. Successful influencers are those who manage to balance monetization efforts with genuine content that truly reflects their values and interests.

In the quest for social media dominance, consistency is key. Whether it's posting schedules or content quality, influencers who maintain consistency are the ones who keep their audience engaged and invested in their journey. This predictability builds a routine for the audience, integrating the influencer's content into their daily lives.

Finally, community building extends beyond the confines of a single platform. Influencers who cultivate communities across various channels enjoy a more resilient and engaged audience base. This multi-platform presence allows them to weather algorithm changes and platform-specific challenges more effectively.

In conclusion, the empire-building journey of influencers on social media is rich with insights and strategies poised to educate and inspire. By delving into their success stories, we uncover a blueprint for viral growth, authentic engagement, and sustained success in the ever-evolving digital realm. As you venture forth, remember that your unique voice, coupled with strategic acumen and unwavering perseverance, is your greatest asset in carving out your own social media empire.

Brands

When we shift the focus from individual influencers to brands, the strategies for building a social media empire take on new dimensions. Brand storytelling becomes paramount, transforming products and services into relatable characters in their own right. Successful brands on social media have mastered the art of weaving their offerings into the fabric of their audience's daily lives, making their presence both indispensable and deeply personal.

Consider the approach of lifestyle and apparel companies that have become household names. They don't just sell products; they sell a lifestyle, a feeling. This is achieved by creating content that resonates on a personal level with their audience. How? Through high-quality visuals, engaging video content, and narratives that speak to the aspirations and challenges of their target market.

Another key strategy is creating a sense of community around the brand. This involves more than just responding to comments or reposting user-generated content. It's about initiating conversations, asking for feedback, and involving the audience in the product development process. By doing so, brands can make their customers feel like they're part of something bigger, fostering loyalty and advocacy.

Let's not forget the power of leveraging social proof. Brands that effectively highlight customer testimonials, user-generated content, and collaborations with influencers can significantly enhance their credibility and reach. This creates a ripple effect, where the engagement from these efforts draws in new audience segments organically.

But successful social media branding isn't just about outward engagement. It's also about deep analytics and understanding the back-end mechanisms of each platform. Brands that excel on social media invest in analyzing their performance data, adjusting their strategies based on insights into what content performs best, when to post it, and how to optimize their ad spend.

Speaking of paid content, a balanced approach between organic and sponsored content is vital. The goal is to ensure that advertisements feel as natural and engaging as the organic content. The brands that do this well seamlessly integrate their paid posts into their narrative, making it hard for the audience to distinguish between what's sponsored and what's not, yet maintaining transparency and trust.

Incentivizing engagement through contests, giveaways, and exclusive offers is another strategy brands use to maintain interest and encourage active participation from their followers. These tactics not only boost engagement rates but also provide valuable user data that can be leveraged for future campaigns.

Adapting to platform changes and algorithm updates is yet another crucial strategy. Brands that remain agile and willing to pivot their content strategies can maintain visibility even as platforms evolve. This might mean embracing new content formats, such as short-form videos or interactive stories, ahead of competitors.

Investing in community management is also essential for brands seeking to build lasting relationships with their audience. This involves more than just moderation; it's about building a rapport with followers, addressing their concerns with empathy, and creating a safe space for dialogue and exchange. This ongoing engagement turns one-time buyers into lifelong fans.

The role of storytelling as a strategy can't be overstated. Brands that succeed on social media are those that tell compelling stories through their posts, stories that align with their brand values and resonate with their audience. This narrative-driven approach helps to differentiate them from competitors and build a unique brand identity.

Leveraging analytics' for content optimization is a game-changer for many brands. By employing data-driven strategies, brands can identify not only what content to produce more of but also the best times to post to maximize engagement. This analytical approach ensures that every piece of content works hard to contribute to the brand's growth.

Moreover, embracing platform diversity is crucial. While it may be tempting for brands to concentrate their efforts on one social media platform, the most successful brands diversify their social media presence. This not only safeguards against the volatility of platform popularity but also enables them to reach different segments of their audience in the environments where they're most engaged.

Collaboration plays a significant role in the expansion of a brand's social media influence. From partnering with influencers for wider reach to collaborating with other brands for cross-promotions, these partnerships can lead to a win-win situation, boosting visibility and engagement for all parties involved.

Finally, a commitment to constant iteration and innovation keeps the social media presence of brands fresh and relevant. The digital landscape is always changing, and so are the preferences of its users. Brands that commit to regularly refining their approach, experimenting with new content types, and staying abreast of digital trends are the ones that thrive in the long term.

In conclusion, the blueprint for building a successful social media empire as a brand hinges on a mix of strategies, from deep engagement and community building to leveraging analytics and embracing platform diversity. By crafting a unique brand story, investing in relationships, and staying adaptable, brands can not only grow their social media presence but turn it into a powerful engine for growth and engagement.

Entrepreneurs

Entrepreneurs are at the forefront of the ever-evolving social media landscape, constantly crafting unique strategies to cut through the noise and connect with their audience. It's not just about promoting a product or service; it's about building an empire that resonates on a personal level with the audience, fostering loyalty and driving engagement. This section explores the journey of entrepreneurs who have mastered the art of social media, turning platforms into powerful tools for growth and monetization.

The essence of success for entrepreneurs on social media lies in understanding the inherent value they offer. It's crucial to identify and hone in on what makes your brand unique. Is it the innovative nature of your products, the story behind your brand, or perhaps the problem-solving capabilities you provide? Identifying this core value is the first step in creating content that not only attracts but also retains attention.

A key aspect of building a successful social media empire as an entrepreneur is the mastery of storytelling. Stories have the power to engage and inspire, making them an invaluable tool in the entrepreneur's arsenal. The most impactful social media empires are built on narratives that people can relate to, see themselves in, and want to be a part of. This emotional investment is what transforms followers into brand ambassadors.

Engagement is the currency of the social media world, and entrepreneurs must be adept at fostering it. This means not just pushing content out, but also pulling insights in. Listening to your audience, understanding their needs, and responding to their feedback are pivotal components. It is this two-way communication that fuels growth and builds a sense of community around your brand.

The algorithms governing social media platforms are often seen as obstacles, but successful entrepreneurs view them as opportunities. By staying informed about how these algorithms work and adjusting your strategy accordingly, you can ensure your content reaches the right eyes at the right time. It's about being adaptable and not shying away from experimenting with new formats or strategies.

Content is undeniably king, but consistency is queen. Consistency in posting not only helps with algorithmic favor but also sets an expectation for your audience. They know they can rely on you for regular updates, which in turn, keeps your brand top of mind. However, it's important to balance quantity with quality. Every post should add value, whether it's through information, inspiration, or entertainment.

The power of leveraging social proof cannot be overstated for entrepreneurs. Sharing customer testimonials, media mentions, or any form of endorsement helps build credibility and trust. It's about showing, not just telling, the world the value of what you offer. User-generated content also plays a crucial role here, serving as authentic proof of your product or service in action.

Networking and collaboration offer another tactical avenue for growth. Connecting with other entrepreneurs, influencers, or brands in your niche for cross-promotion or collaborations can expose your brand to a broader audience. It's a win-win scenario that, when executed thoughtfully, can lead to significant increases in followers and engagement.

Monetization is, of course, a critical part of scaling your social media empire. Whether it's through partnerships with brands, selling merchandise, or offering exclusive content through subscription models, entrepreneurs need to think creatively about revenue streams. Diversifying your income ensures sustainability and supports continued growth.

Analyzing your performance through analytics is akin to a feedback loop for continuous improvement. Metrics provide insights into what's working and what isn't, enabling you to refine your strategy over time. This data-driven approach ensures that you're not just throwing content out into the void but are making informed decisions that contribute to your growth.

Adaptability is essential in an environment as dynamic as social media. Trends change, algorithms get updated, and audience preferences evolve. Successful entrepreneurs stay ahead of the curve by being flexible and willing to pivot their strategies as needed. They keep an eye on future trends and are always prepared to incorporate new ideas to stay relevant and engaging.

Another pivotal aspect of building a social media empire is focusing on community building. It's about fostering an environment where your followers feel valued and heard. Community-led initiatives, such as exclusive groups or forums, can enhance engagement and loyalty. The goal is to create a space where your audience can connect not just with your brand, but with each other.

In the journey to social media success, resilience is key. Challenges such as negative feedback, growth plateaus, or algorithm changes are inevitable. The entrepreneurs who thrive are those who see these challenges as opportunities for learning and growth. It's about remaining committed to your vision, even when the going gets tough.

Lastly, never underestimate the importance of authenticity. In a world saturated with content, authenticity stands out. It's the genuine passion for what you do that will resonate with people. Successful entrepreneurs don't just sell a product or service; they share a piece of themselves with the world. It's this personal touch that truly transforms a brand into an empire.

In conclusion, building a successful social media empire as an entrepreneur is a multifaceted journey. It requires a deep understanding of your brand's value, mastery of storytelling, engagement, algorithm optimization, consistency, credibility, collaboration, inventive monetization, analytical rigor, adaptability, community focus, resilience, and above all, authenticity. By embracing these principles, entrepreneurs can not only achieve social media success but also make a lasting impact on their audience.

Chapter 11:
Future Trends in Social Media

As we pivot to the future of social media, it's essential to keep a keen eye on emerging platforms and the evolving role of AI and technology, ensuring our strategies stay ahead of the curve. The digital landscape is morphing at breakneck speed, with new platforms emerging that could be the next big avenue for growth and monetization. Understanding these platforms and integrating them into your social media empire early on can give you a significant edge. Equally crucial is grasping the potential of AI and technology in crafting more engaging, personalized content, and analyzing data to make informed strategic decisions. Moreover, as consumption patterns shift, adapting your content to meet these changes will be pivotal. The integration of virtual and augmented reality into social media offers an untapped well of opportunities for immersive storytelling, potentially revolutionizing engagement. Staying adaptable, embracing technological advancements, and experimenting with new formats will be your compass to navigating the ever-changing terrain of social media.

Emerging Platforms to Watch

As we dive into the crux of identifying tomorrow's social media giants, it's essential to focus on those emerging platforms that exhibit unique attributes, promising a fertile ground for virality, growth, and potentially massive financial returns. These platforms, by virtue of their novelty, come with less competition and open the door to innovative content strategies that might not thrive on more established networks.

One such platform, rapidly gaining traction, is Vero. Vero stands out by promising a more authentic social experience, free of ads and algorithms that dictate what you see. For content creators, this means a straightforward relationship with your audience, where engagement is driven purely by interest rather than algorithmic preference. The potential here is vast for those who can build a strong follower base early on.

Another platform worth noting is Caffeine. Originally tailored for gamers and sports enthusiasts, Caffeine is expanding its horizon to include all sorts of live broadcasts. What makes it an enticing option for content creators is its real-time interaction capabilities, which profoundly enhance audience engagement and offer a more dynamic interaction model than static posts or delayed comments.

Substack, while primarily a newsletter platform, is shaping up to be a significant player in the social media landscape. It provides a direct line to your audience's inbox, which, in an age where attention is a scarce commodity, is incredibly valuable. For those looking to monetize their content or brand, Substack offers straightforward subscription models that are lucrative and build a sense of community among your readership.

Clubhouse had its moment of explosive growth, highlighting the untapped market for audio-only platforms. While its initial blaze of publicity has cooled, the platform's concept has proven enduring. The intimate nature of voice and the platform's networking capabilities make it an intriguing space for creating a unique personal brand and establishing yourself as a thought leader in your niche.

While not entirely new, Twitch's continued evolution beyond gaming presents new opportunities. Its livestreaming capabilities, coupled with a highly engaged audience, offer a ripe environment for creative content that can captivate viewers for longer spans, proving advantageous for building a loyal community and enhancing your content's reach.

Dispo, a photo-sharing app, brings a novel twist by reintroducing the anticipation of waiting to see photos until they "develop" the next day. This nostalgia-infused approach coupled with a strong emphasis on authentic, in-the-moment content, offers a fresh angle for content creation that can stand out amidst the polished, curated feeds on other platforms.

Understanding the unique proposition of each of these platforms is just the first step. The next, and perhaps most crucial, is crafting a content strategy that plays to their strengths. This requires a keen sense of creativity and a willingness to experiment and adapt.

For instance, leveraging Vero's ad-free experience means cultivating organic growth through quality content alone, a challenge that encourages genuine creativity and value-driven posts. On Caffeine, the real-time interaction demands a level of spontaneity and the ability to engage an audience live, skills that can be honed but are immensely rewarding.

Substack's model prioritizes depth over breadth. Success here depends on consistently delivering value-packed content that justifies a subscription. It's about fostering loyalty and establishing a direct relationship with your audience that translates to sustainable revenue.

On platforms like Clubhouse, the key lies in engaging in meaningful conversations and sharing insights that showcase your expertise. Building your brand here means being both a listener and a contributor, leveraging the power of spoken words to connect and persuade.

For Twitch, it's about extending the platform's inherent entertainment value. Whether it's through gaming, cooking, or just casual chats, the aim is to make each stream an event that viewers look forward to, blending entertainment with a touch of personal connection.

Dispo's unique selling point of authenticity and nostalgia can be a breath of fresh air for audiences bombarded with curated content. It calls for a return to the spontaneity that first made social media so compelling, offering an avenue to stand out by embracing the imperfections that make experiences genuine.

Beyond just understanding these platforms, success also hinges on constantly keeping an ear to the ground for shifts in social media trends, audience preferences, and platform features. It's a dynamic landscape, and flexibility in adapting your strategy is crucial.

Moreover, these platforms offer an opportunity to redefine what social media means to you and your audience. They challenge the norm, inviting content creators to be pioneers in shaping the culture of new digital spaces. It's about carving out a niche that resonates with your unique voice and vision.

Ultimately, thriving on these emerging platforms requires a blend of creativity, adaptability, and foresight. It's about recognizing the potential in these nascent spaces and seizing the opportunity to grow alongside them. As the digital sphere continues to evolve, staying ahead means being open to exploring uncharted territories, always ready to adapt and innovate. The potential is limitless for those willing to dive in and navigate these exciting new waters.

The Role of AI and Technology

In the dynamic world of social media, the cutting edge is constantly being reshaped by rapid advancements in AI and technology. These tools aren't just accessories; they're integral to how content creators can grow their audiences, go viral, and monetize their presence more effectively than ever before. Understanding the role of AI and technology is not just beneficial—it's essential for staying ahead in the game.

First off, algorithms powered by AI are the gatekeepers of visibility on most platforms. Every like, share, or comment is analyzed to determine what content gets promoted. This means creators need to master the nuances of these algorithms. By diving into analytics, you can identify the type of content that resonates with your audience, helping you craft posts that are more likely to get picked up and featured prominently.

AI doesn't stop at algorithms, though. It extends into content creation itself. Tools like automated video editors or AI-based writing assistants can massively reduce the time it takes to produce content. This allows creators to focus on ideation and strategy, rather than getting bogged down in the minutiae of content production. The key is to leverage these tools to enhance creativity, not replace it.

Chatbots and AI-driven customer service tools are revolutionizing the way creators engage with their followers. They provide instant responses to common queries, freeing up time for you to engage in more meaningful interactions. This kind of efficiency boosts audience satisfaction and fosters a deeper sense of community around your brand.

Personalization is another area where AI is making big waves. By analyzing data on viewer preferences and behaviors, AI can help tailor your content to suit different segments of your audience. This means your posts will have a greater impact, driving up engagement rates and fostering a closer connection with your followers.

One of the most exciting applications of AI in social media is in predictive analysis. AI can forecast trends and help you jump on them before they go mainstream. This predictive capability means you can produce content that's ahead of the curve, positioning you as a thought leader in your niche.

Content moderation is a less glamorous but equally important application of AI. It helps in identifying and filtering out inappropriate or harmful content. For creators, this means maintaining a clean and positive space for your community, aligning with the values and standards you want to uphold.

Augmented Reality (AR) and Virtual Reality (VR) are setting new standards for immersive content. These technologies allow you to create experiences that engage your audience in novel and captivating ways. From virtual try-ons for fashion influencers to immersive tours for travel bloggers, the possibilities are endless.

AI-generated content is a burgeoning field that presents both opportunities and challenges. While it can provide personalized content at scale, there's a fine line between use and misuse. Authenticity is key in social media, so it's crucial to strike the right balance between AI-generated and human-created content.

The role of technology in analytics cannot be overstated. With advanced tools at your disposal, you can delve deep into data, gaining insights that inform your content strategy. From identifying the best time to post to understanding the intricacies of audience demographics, data analytics is your roadmap to success.

Looking forward, the integration of AI and technology in social media is set to deepen. We're likely to see even more sophisticated tools for content creation, audience engagement, and analytics. Staying abreast of these developments and learning how to leverage them will be vital.

However, amidst this tech-driven evolution, the human element remains paramount. Technology is a tool, but creativity, empathy, and genuine human connection are the heart of any successful social media strategy. Blending the power of AI with the unique touch of human creativity is where the magic happens.

For those looking to capitalize on these trends, continuous learning and experimentation are key. Test new tools, analyze their impact, and always keep your audience's preferences at the forefront. Remember, the goal of leveraging AI and technology is to amplify your reach and engagement, making your social media platforms more vibrant and valuable to your followers.

As we gaze into the future of social media, it's clear that AI and technology will be central to shaping its landscape. They offer unprecedented opportunities for creators to innovate, personalize, and connect. By embracing these tools, you can elevate your social media presence, enchant your audience, and achieve your growth and monetization goals.

In closing, as you venture into the evolving social media terrain, let AI and technology be your allies. Harness their potential to create compelling content, engage deeply with your community, and turn your social media platforms into thriving empires. The future is bright, and the tools at your disposal are more powerful than ever—use them wisely.

Adapting to Changes in Social Media Consumption

In the dynamic landscape of social media, adapting to shifts in user behavior and platform algorithms is not just beneficial; it's necessary for survival and growth. As we navigate through the kaleidoscopic world of likes, shares, and viral content, understanding how to pivot in response to these changes can be the difference between obscurity and fame.

First and foremost, it's imperative to keep a finger on the pulse of emerging trends. Social media consumption is not static; it evolves with cultural shifts, technological advancements, and user preferences. Today's leading platforms may become tomorrow's digital relics, and the content that resonates now might not hold the same appeal in the future.

To stay ahead, constantly research and engage with new platforms and tools. For instance, the rise of short video content a la TikTok has revolutionized social media consumption, pushing creators to think succinctly and engage viewers in seconds. Being an early adopter of emerging platforms can give you a strategic advantage, providing access to an untapped audience eager for fresh content.

Another critical factor is the understanding of analytics. Deep diving into your social media metrics isn't just number crunching; it's a roadmap to what your audience enjoys. Pay attention to the type of content that drives engagement, the time of day when your posts receive the most attention, and the demographics of your most active followers. This data is invaluable when adjusting your content strategy to align with changing consumption patterns.

Engagement is the currency of social media, and fostering a community around your brand or persona is essential. As social media platforms introduce new features for interaction, such as Instagram's "Stories" or Twitter's "Spaces," it's crucial to incorporate these into your engagement strategy. Actively participating in these spaces can significantly increase your visibility and strengthen your connection with your audience.

Content diversification is another key tactic. While having a niche is important, experimenting with different content formats can reveal new avenues for growth. If you primarily post photos, try integrating video content. If you're known for serious topics, sprinkle in some humor or lighthearted posts. This not only keeps your current audience engaged but can also attract new followers looking for that type of content.

Remember, the algorithms are always watching. Platforms prioritize content that keeps users engaged and on the app for longer. Understanding the intricacies of these algorithms can help you tailor your content for better visibility. Whether it's posting at optimal times, using the right hashtags, or leveraging platform-specific features, aligning your strategy with the algorithms can amplify your reach exponentially.

Collaborations and partnerships continue to be a powerful tool for adapting to changes in social media consumption. Teaming up with other creators or brands can introduce your content to a broader audience. It's also an excellent way to create fresh and engaging content that can captivate both your existing audience and your partner's audience.

Listening to your audience is more than just monitoring comments and messages. It's about understanding their evolving needs and interests. Conduct surveys, ask for feedback, and create content that addresses their desires. Your audience's preferences can change, and staying attuned to these changes keeps your content relevant and engaging.

Investing in continued learning can't be overstated. The world of social media is vast, with endless resources available to help you sharpen your skills. Online courses, webinars, podcasts, and books by industry leaders can provide insights into adapting strategies and staying innovative.

Flexibility and resilience are qualities every successful social media influencer shares. Algorithm changes, platform updates, and shifting user behaviors can disrupt even the most well-thought-out strategies.

Being prepared to pivot and adapt your approach is crucial for long-term success.

Don't overlook the importance of authenticity. In a space crowded with curated content and polished personas, being genuine can set you apart. Adapting doesn't mean losing your unique voice; it's about evolving while staying true to what makes your content distinctly yours.

In conclusion, adapting to changes in social media consumption demands a multifaceted approach. It's about staying informed, being flexible, and maintaining a deep connection with your audience. As you evolve your strategies, keep your focus on creating content that resonates, engages, and entertains. The landscape of social media might be constantly changing, but by being proactive and prepared to adapt, you can not only survive but thrive.

As we look towards the future, one thing is clear: the need to adapt will never change. Embrace it, and see every shift in social media consumption as an opportunity to innovate and grow your social media presence. With the right mindset and strategies, the changing tides of social media can lead you to new heights of success and influence.

Now, as we continue to chart your path through the world of social media, remember that the journey is as dynamic as the platforms themselves. Adaptation is not just a strategy; it's a mindset. Equip yourself with it, and you're well on your way to mastering the ever-evolving landscape of social media.

Chapter 12:
Personal Branding and Social Media

As we pivot from the overarching strategy of viral growth and engagement, it's time to dive deep into the essence of personal branding within the social media universe. The impact of your personal brand extends far beyond just a recognizable logo or a catchy tagline; it's about curating an authentic experience that resonates with your audience on a personal level. In this realm, consistency isn't just a buzzword—it's your best friend. Think of your social media channels as a canvas, and your personal brand as the palette of colors you choose to paint with. Every post, story, and tweet is a stroke of paint that contributes to a larger masterpiece that is uniquely yours. The magic happens when your followers can glance at a piece of content and immediately know it's yours, even before seeing your name. This chapter explores how to craft a cohesive personal brand that aligns with your goals, engages your target audience, and positions you as a thought leader in your niche. We'll tackle the intricacies of brand voice, aesthetics, and the storytelling techniques that can make your personal brand not just seen, but felt. Here, you'll learn how to transform your personal brand into a magnet that not only attracts followers but turns them into loyal advocates for your mission. Remember, in the ever-evolving landscape of social media, your personal brand is the anchor that keeps your strategy grounded.

Creating a Cohesive Personal Brand

When diving deep into the realm of personal branding on social media, it's crucial to understand that a cohesive personal brand is your digital fingerprint. It's not just about matching colors or having a catchy tagline; it's about crafting an identity that resonates with your audience, is consistent across all platforms, and delivers a unique and memorable experience. This cohesive brand becomes your calling card in the vast world of social media.

First, consider the foundation of your personal brand. Ask yourself what you stand for, what values you hold dear, and what message you want to convey to your audience. These elements are the essence of your brand and should be evident in every piece of content you share. Your personal brand's foundation is what sets you apart from the masses and attracts your ideal audience to you.

Visual consistency plays a pivotal role in creating a cohesive personal brand. This means using consistent color schemes, fonts, and imagery across all your social media platforms. This visual consistency helps in reinforcing your brand identity and makes your content instantly recognizable to your followers, no matter where they see it.

However, a cohesive personal brand isn't just about aesthetics. Your voice and tone are just as important. Whether you're informative, witty, or inspirational, your way of expressing should remain consistent. It's how people come to recognize and trust your communications. This doesn't mean you can't explore different facets of your personality, but there should be a consistent undertone that your audience can come to expect and relate to.

Content congruency is another critical aspect. Your posts, regardless of the platform, should align with your overall brand message and goals. If you're a fitness enthusiast advocating for a healthy lifestyle, it wouldn't make sense to suddenly flood your feed with fast food promotions. Stay true to your brand's core message, and make sure your content supports your brand's mission.

Engagement strategy also plays into your personal brand. The way you interact with your followers, the content you choose to engage with, and even the timing of your posts contribute to the perception of your brand. Authentic engagement not only builds trust but also strengthens your brand community.

Storytelling is an immensely powerful tool in personal branding. Your audience isn't just looking for products or services; they're looking for a narrative they can connect with. Share your journey, your wins, and even your failures. This vulnerability and authenticity forge deeper connections and make your personal brand more relatable.

Consistency in posting is not to be overlooked. A well-maintained content calendar that showcases consistent themes, topics, and posting schedules helps in keeping your audience engaged and reinforces your brand presence. It's a balance between being predictable in your reliability but surprising in your content delivery.

Remember, personal branding on social media is not a one-size-fits-all scenario. What works for one brand may not work for yours. Experimentation within the bounds of your brand identity is crucial. Analyze your analytics, see what resonates with your audience, and don't be afraid to refine your approach.

User feedback is a goldmine for personal branding. Listening to your audience can provide insights into what aspects of your brand they love and what could be improved. This feedback loop can help you fine-tune your brand to better serve your audience's needs.

Incorporating your personal interests and hobbies can add a unique flavor to your brand. These aspects make your brand more human and approachable. It shows your audience that there's a real person behind the brand, not just a content-producing machine.

A critical but often overlooked aspect of personal branding is network building. Collaborating with other content creators not only exposes you to a broader audience but also aligns your brand with others that share similar values and audiences. This synergy can significantly amplify your brand's reach and recognition.

Adaptability is key in maintaining a cohesive personal brand. Social media trends and platform algorithms are constantly changing. Your ability to adapt your brand messaging and content strategy while staying true to your core identity is crucial for long-term success.

Finally, remember that building a cohesive personal brand is a journey, not a destination. It requires patience, consistency, and genuine passion for your niche. As you grow and evolve, so will your brand. Stay true to your core values, and don't be afraid to let your brand reflect your evolution.

In conclusion, a cohesive personal brand on social media is a powerful tool for anyone looking to go viral, monetize their presence, and create a lasting impact. It's about much more than just aesthetics; it's about crafting an identity that resonates authenticity, consistency, and value to your audience. With the right approach, your personal brand can become a beacon for followers, collaborators, and opportunities alike.

The Impact of Personal Branding on Growth

Personal branding isn't just a buzzword. In the ecosystem of social media, it's an essential strategy that could mean the difference between languishing in obscurity and reaching viral success. Embracing personal branding is akin to setting the stage for your online presence, where authenticity and consistency paint the picture of who you are and what you stand for. But what's often overlooked is its profound impact on growth, a factor critical for anyone looking to make a mark on social media.

Imagine personal branding as your digital footprint; it's unique to you. Just as every tweet, post, or video contributes to this footprint, each also has the potential to magnetically attract followers. This attraction isn't by chance. It stems from a congruent narrative that resonates with your audience. They're not just following a profile—they're connecting with a person whose values, content, and vision align with their own. It's this personal connection that accelerates growth.

But here's a caveat: personal branding isn't a 'set and forget' deal. It's an ongoing process of refinement and evolution. It demands an understanding of not just where you are currently, but where you aim to be. This forward-thinking approach encourages adaptability—an essential trait for navigating the ever-changing landscapes of social media platforms.

Dig a layer deeper, and you'll find that personal branding is also about perception. How do viewers perceive you? Do they see a leader, an innovator, or an inspirer? This perception directly influences your social media growth. A strong, positive perception can propel you toward opportunities - collaborations, partnerships, and even sponsorships. Each of these opportunities is a stepping stone to amplify your reach and, subsequently, your growth.

Then, there's the algorithm. Love it or loathe it, understanding and leveraging the algorithm of each social media platform is pivotal. What many don't realize is that personal branding can actually work in harmony with these algorithms. Algorithms favor engagement; a personalized, authentic brand naturally fosters a higher level of interaction and engagement, thereby favoring your content in the vast sea of posts.

Another aspect to consider is competition. In an arena as saturated as social media, standing out is no small feat. Personal branding is your armor and sword in this battle. It's what makes you recognizable in the throng, carving out a niche that's uniquely yours. This distinction is not merely for vanity's sake—it's a strategic move towards securing your spot in the feeds and hearts of your target audience.

Now, consider the concept of social proof. When your personal brand begins to grow, it establishes you as a figure of authority in your niche. This authority isn't just ceremonial. It's a beacon that signals trust, reliability, and respect. As your personal brand garners this social proof, growth becomes a natural progression. People are drawn to authority figures in their community, and social media is no exception.

Let's talk about the multiplier effect of a strong personal brand on growth. Each piece of content you share isn't merely consumed; it's a potential share, a potential discussion point, and a potential connection. This multiplied effect is exponential in nature. As your brand's visibility increases, so does the potential for virality. The essence of viral content isn't just in its appeal but in its shareability—a direct offshoot of a compelling personal brand.

But perhaps the most significant impact of personal branding on growth is its role in building a community. Beyond numbers and algorithms, social media is fundamentally about people and connections. A personal brand that places community at its heart is poised for organic growth. This isn't growth that's bought or artificially inflated; it's growth that's nurtured, one genuine connection at a time.

Moreover, personal branding allows for an elevated level of storytelling. Each post, each campaign, and each interaction is a chapter in your story. People aren't just attracted to content; they're attracted to narratives. The cohesion and relatability of your personal brand's narrative can significantly enhance engagement, driving growth through storytelling that connects and resonates.

Yet, it's crucial to note the role of consistency in personal branding. Consistency isn't just about posting regularly; it's about maintaining the core essence of your personal brand across all platforms and interactions. This consistency builds recognition, fosters trust, and simplifies the journey of your audience through the different stages of growth, from awareness to advocacy.

Engagement is another cornerstone of growth, and here too, personal branding plays a pivotal role. An authentic personal brand encourages open dialogue, questions, and community participation. This level of engagement not only boosts visibility but also deepens relationships with your audience, laying the groundwork for sustained growth.

In navigating the journey of personal branding, it's essential to leverage feedback and analytics. These insights are invaluable in understanding what resonates with your audience and what doesn't. Adjusting your personal brand based on this feedback isn't about losing authenticity; it's about evolving in a way that serves both you and your community better.

Importantly, personal branding opens the door to diversification. As your brand grows, so do the opportunities to branch out into different platforms, mediums, and ventures. This diversification isn't just a safeguard against the whims of algorithm changes; it's a strategy to capture broader audiences and ensure robust growth.

Finally, the impact of personal branding on growth is a testament to the power of human connection in the digital age. It's a reminder that at the core of every like, share, and follow is a person seeking connection, value, and community. Personal branding, when embraced with authenticity and strategic acumen, holds the key to unlocking this potential for growth. It's not just about being seen; it's about being remembered, respected, and revered.

In the tapestry of social media, personal branding is your thread. Weave it with intention, creativity, and authenticity, and watch as it transforms the canvas of your online presence, driving growth that's both meaningful and monumental.

Chapter 13:
Legal and Ethical Considerations

In carving your path to social media stardom, it's paramount not to overlook the legal landmines and ethical tightropes that could potentially derail your journey. This chapter delves into critical aspects like copyright and fair use, underscored by the reality that what you share and how you share it matters immensely. Imagine finding the perfect image or clip that complements your content, only to face legal repercussions for not securing the right permissions. Similarly, privacy and data protection are no less significant, especially in an era where personal information is as valuable as currency. Protecting your accounts from hacking goes beyond simple password practices; it encompasses a broader understanding of digital hygiene to safeguard not just your information, but also your followers'. Moreover, the ethics of influencer marketing highlight the importance of transparency and honesty in your endorsements. Your audience trusts you, and misleading them for short-term gains can tarnish your reputation irreversibly. As we navigate these legal and ethical considerations, remember that they are not just hurdles, but foundational pillars that ensure your empire not only grows but thrives on integrity and respect.

Copyright and Fair Use

As we venture deeper into the thrilling world of social media stardom, it's critical to navigate the legal frameworks that surround the content we create and share. Copyright and fair use aren't just legalese—they're essential guidelines that protect creators while enabling innovation and expression. Understand these concepts well, and you'll steer clear of potentially disastrous pitfalls while nurturing your growth and creativity.

Copyright is the cornerstone of creative protection. It automatically safeguards original works of authorship, including literary, dramatic, musical, and certain other intellectual works, the moment they're fixed in a tangible medium of expression. This means your unique blog posts, mesmerizing photos, captivating videos, and snappy tweets are protected by copyright law as soon as they exist in a form that can be perceived, reproduced, or otherwise communicated.

However, the digital landscape is a remix culture. We often want to use existing content—be it a trending music clip, an iconic movie scene, or a viral meme—as a foundation or accent within our own creations. This is where fair use comes into play. Fair use is a legal doctrine that allows limited use of copyrighted material without requiring permission from the rights holders, especially for purposes such as commentary, criticism, news reporting, teaching, scholarship, and research.

Understanding the nuances of fair use can be tricky. It involves balancing four key factors: the purpose and character of your use, the nature of the copyrighted work, the amount and substantiality of the portion taken, and the effect of the use on the potential market for the original work. Transformative uses that add new expression or meaning and don't compete with the original work are more likely to be considered fair use.

But here's the kicker: there's no surefire formula to determine fair use. Courts assess it on a case-by-case basis, which means your interpretation of fair use might differ from someone else's—and ultimately from a legal ruling. To play it safe, ask yourself whether your content could exist without the copyrighted material. If it can't, ensure your use strongly leans into purposes recognized under fair use, like parody, criticism, or educational commentary.

When in doubt, seek permission. Reaching out to copyright holders for consent to use their materials can safeguard you against infringement claims. Many creators are open to collaboration or can agree on a licensing fee. Additionally, leverage the wealth of royalty-free resources available online; numerous sites offer high-quality images, videos, and music that can elevate your content without risking infringement.

Creative Commons licenses are another crucial element in the mix. These licenses enable creators to communicate which rights they reserve and which they waive for the benefit of other creators. Using content under Creative Commons licenses can significantly widen your creative horizons, as long as you adhere to the conditions set by the copyright holder.

Remember, the line between inspiration and infringement can be finer than you think. If your content significantly relies on someone else's copyrighted work, that's a clear red flag. Develop a keen sense of when to dial back or pivot your approach to stay on the right side of copyright law.

Digital platforms also have their mechanisms to protect copyright and manage claims. Familiarize yourself with the copyright policies of the social media platforms you use most often. Many have automated systems, like YouTube's Content ID, to detect and manage copyright infringement. Being aware of these systems can help you navigate claims, whether you're disputing one or filing it yourself.

Documentation and meticulous record-keeping can be your best allies, especially if you frequently license content or secure permissions. Maintain a clear record of your licenses and permissions, as well as any correspondence related to copyright clearance. This documentation can be vital in defending your use as lawful should disputes arise.

Moreover, consider investing in copyright education. Several online courses and resources can deepen your understanding of copyright law, making you more confident in your content creation journey. Knowledge is power, and in the fast-evolving world of social media, staying informed is non-negotiable.

Lastly, respect for copyright signals respect for fellow creators. It's about fostering a community where creativity can flourish without fear of being undermined or appropriated unjustly. As you aspire to viral success, remember that sustainable growth and respect in the digital sphere come from nurturing an environment of mutual respect and legal awareness.

In conclusion, navigating the complexities of copyright and fair use is a critical aspect of building and protecting your social media empire. By understanding and respecting these legal frameworks, you're not just avoiding potential legal hurdles—you're also honoring the broader community of creators. Empower yourself with knowledge, use resources wisely, and always aim to contribute positively to the rich tapestry of digital expression.

Privacy and Data Protection

In today's digital age, privacy and data protection have become hot topics, especially for those looking to make waves on social media platforms. As you focus on growing, monetizing, and going viral, it's crucial to understand the legal and ethical implications surrounding your and your audience's data. This understanding will not only help protect your empire but also build trust within your community.

Firstly, the essence of privacy in social media is understanding what information you're sharing, both willingly and unknowingly. Every platform has its unique set of privacy policies and terms of service. It's a no-brainer, yet many overlook the importance of thoroughly reading these documents before diving in. This foundational step ensures you're aware of how platforms use your content and personal data.

Data protection is another crucial aspect. It encompasses measures and policies you implement to safeguard your personal data and the information you collect from your followers. This is where encryption, secure passwords, and two-factor authentication aren't just buzzwords but necessities. They are the first line of defense against unwelcome intruders, ensuring your digital footprint remains yours and yours alone.

Understanding the concept of data minimization can also greatly enhance your privacy strategy. This means you only collect the essential data needed from your audience. Not only does this simplify data management, but it also minimizes the risk of breaching privacy regulations. Remember, in the realm of data, more isn't always better.

Incorporating privacy policies on any platform you use for business is a must. These policies should be accessible, easy to understand, and transparent. They detail how you collect, use, protect, and share data. This transparency isn't just about legal compliance; it's about showing your followers that you value and protect their privacy.

Now, given the rapid pace of technological advancement, staying informed about privacy laws and regulations is vital. Laws such as the General Data Protection Regulation (GDPR) in Europe and the California Consumer Privacy Act (CCPA) in the U.S. could have profound implications on how you manage your social media platforms. Non-compliance can result in hefty fines and, worse, a tarnished reputation.

Consent is a cornerstone of data protection. Whether it's sending newsletters, using cookies on your website, or sharing user-generated content, obtaining explicit permission from your audience is non-negotiable. This not only respects their privacy but also fortifies your integrity as a trustworthy influencer or brand.

While it might seem daunting, managing data protection doesn't have to be a solo journey. Leveraging tools and resources designed for data privacy can streamline the process. From compliance checklists to encryption tools, there's a plethora of options available to ensure you're on the right track.

One often overlooked aspect is the personal touch in communication about privacy. Yes, privacy policies and terms of service are inherently legal documents, but that doesn't mean they should be impenetrable. Simplifying the language and making these documents relatable and understandable will go a long way in gaining your audience's trust.

Audit your data practices regularly. The digital landscape is always changing, and what worked a year ago might not be sufficient today. Regular audits of how you collect, store, and handle data ensure you remain compliant and secure. Plus, it sends a clear message to your followers that their privacy is a top priority.

Regarding your audience's data, transparency is key. Be open about what data you're collecting and why. If your followers understand the value exchange – for example, personalizing their experience on your platform – they're more likely to trust you with their information. This trust is the bedrock of any successful social media presence.

Don't forget the power of educating your audience on privacy. Sharing tips and best practices for data protection not only helps them safeguard their own privacy but also reinforces your position as a responsible influencer or brand. This educational approach can differentiate you in a crowded digital space.

Lastly, remember that privacy and data protection aren't just about avoiding legal pitfalls; they're about respect. Respecting your data, respecting your audience's data, and respecting the laws designed to protect that data. This respect forms the foundation of a sustainable, trust-based relationship with your followers, which is invaluable in the social media world.

In conclusion, privacy and data protection are crucial considerations for anyone looking to succeed on social media. By implementing sound privacy policies, respecting data laws, and fostering an environment of trust and transparency, you can protect your digital empire while building a loyal and engaged following. Let the principles of privacy and protection guide you as you navigate the complex yet rewarding landscape of social media.

As we move forward, remember that privacy isn't just a set of rules to follow; it's a commitment to integrity, respect, and community building. With these principles in mind, you're well on your way to not only achieving viral success but also establishing a lasting, impactful presence on social media.

Protecting Your Accounts From Hacking In the current digital world, your social media profiles are not just platforms for sharing content but are also valuable assets in your pursuit to grow, monetize, and create a lasting impact. However, as your visibility and influence expand, so does the target on your back for potential hackers. Let's dive into actionable strategies to bulletproof your accounts against unauthorized access, ensuring your empire remains unbreachable.

First and foremost, the cornerstone of account security is a strong, unique password. It sounds like a basic step, yet many fall into the trap of using easily guessable passwords or, worse, the same password across multiple platforms. Invest in a password manager to generate and store complex passwords. This alone significantly reduces the risk of hacking.

Next up, enable two-factor authentication (2FA) wherever possible. A lot of social media platforms now offer this feature. 2FA adds an additional layer of security by requiring a second form of verification beyond your password, often a code sent to your mobile device. This means even if someone gets hold of your password, they won't easily access your account without this second code.

Be wary of phishing attempts. Hackers often use sophisticated phishing emails or messages that mimic those from legitimate sources, luring you into providing your login details. Always double-check the URL and the sender's email address. When in doubt, instead of clicking on any links, directly navigate to the social media platform through your browser or official app.

Regularly review the third-party apps connected to your social media accounts. These apps can often have permissions that include accessing and managing your account. If you don't recognize an app or no longer use it, revoke its access. This is a simple yet effective way to minimize vulnerabilities.

Consider using a dedicated device for managing your social media accounts. This might seem a bit over the top, but it's a strategy used by individuals and businesses that handle highly sensitive information. By limiting the activities and software installed on this device, you reduce the risk of accidental downloads of malware or spyware that could compromise your accounts.

Update your security settings and software regularly. Social media platforms frequently update their security features to combat new hacking techniques. By keeping your app and device software up to date, you close off vulnerabilities that hackers exploit.

Create a routine to check your accounts for unusual activity. This could be new posts you didn't make, messages you didn't send, or new follows or likes to unknown accounts. Early detection of these signs can be crucial in recovering your account before significant damage is done.

Educate yourself about the latest hacking trends and security measures. Cybersecurity is an ever-evolving field, and staying informed about new threats and protection strategies is vital. Platforms like Twitter, Instagram, and Facebook often share updates on new security features and recommended practices for users.

In conclusion, as you embark on your journey to social media fame and fortune, don't let the fear of hacking hold you back. By taking proactive steps to secure your accounts, you're not just protecting your digital assets but also ensuring the trust and safety of your community. Remember, in the digital realm, your security practices are as crucial as the content you create.

The Ethics of Influencer Marketing

In today's digital age, influencer marketing has become a cornerstone of brand promotion and audience engagement on social media. However, this surge in influencer collaborations comes with a significant need for ethical scrutiny. As you navigate the sprawling landscape of social media with ambitions to grow, monetize, and potentially go viral, understanding the ethical implications behind influencer marketing is not just important—it's critical.

Transparency is the bedrock of ethical influencer marketing. Audiences today are savvy; they can detect insincerity from miles away. When an influencer partners with a brand, disclosing this relationship is not only a legal requirement in many jurisdictions but also a practice that fosters trust. A simple #ad or #sponsored can go a long way in maintaining transparency. This practice ensures your followers know when content is sponsored, allowing them to form their own opinions about the authenticity of your recommendation.

Authenticity, while somewhat nebulous, is equally pivotal. The digital persona you cultivate and the partnerships you choose should align with your personal brand and values. Authentic partnerships resonate well with audiences, as they are based on genuine appreciation and use of the products or services being promoted. This authentic approach not only enhances credibility but also fosters a deeper connection with your audience.

Alongside transparency and authenticity, respecting your audience's privacy is a cornerstone of ethical influencer marketing. In the pursuit of personalization, the line between engaging content and intrusive overreach can sometimes blur. Ethical influencers respect this boundary, ensuring that content creation and audience interaction never compromise the privacy or security of their followers.

Financial ethics also play a significant role in the realm of influencer marketing. This includes fair compensation for collaborations and honesty about the potential financial outcomes of promoted investment opportunities or products. Misleading your audience about the potential gains from a product or service can have serious repercussions, not just for your followers, but for your reputation and potentially your legal standing.

In dealing with negative feedback, an ethical influencer responds with grace and accountability. It's easy to bask in the glow of positive engagement, but how you handle criticism or dissatisfaction says volumes about your integrity. Addressing concerns directly, correcting misinformation, and learning from feedback are practices that bolster trust and demonstrate a commitment to your audience's well-being.

Meanwhile, the issue of content originality cannot be overlooked. With the vast amount of content available, ensuring that your work is original or properly credited is essential. This isn't just about legal compliance; it's a matter of respecting fellow creators and acknowledging their contributions to the digital landscape.

Another area that requires ethical reflection is the impact of your content. In your quest to go viral or engage your audience, it's crucial to ponder the wider social and psychological effects. This means avoiding content that perpetuates stereotypes, spreads misinformation, or could be harmful to specific groups. The power of influence is substantial, and wielding it responsibly can contribute to a more informed, respectful, and empathetic online community.

Lastly, for those who manage to climb the lofty heights of social media influence, there's an inherent responsibility to give back. Whether through charity, raising awareness on critical issues, or simply by inspiring others, leveraging your platform for positive change can leave a lasting legacy beyond likes and shares.

As you venture forth in your social media journey, remember that ethics in influencer marketing isn't just about navigating legal landmines. It's about forging genuine connections, fostering trust, and creating value that resonates with your audience on a profound level. Through ethical practices, your influence can become not just widespread, but deeply impactful.

Chapter 14:
Creating a Lasting Impact

In this digital age, where trends can disappear as quickly as they arrive, the aspiration to create a lasting impact through your social media platforms takes more than just surface-level engagement; it demands depth, purpose, and a relentless drive to inspire change. Holding true to the essence of virality, the power of social media doesn't just lie in the number of likes or shares but in its unparalleled capability to mobilize communities, champion causes, and create tangible action in the world. It's about weaving a narrative that transcends the digital realm, transforming passive observers into active participants in a shared vision. To embark on this journey, one must first recognize that authenticity becomes the backbone of any influential campaign. It isn't enough to spark a conversation; you must nourish it, encouraging sustained dialogue that fosters a sense of belonging amongst your followers. As we delve deeper, the importance of building a purpose-driven community becomes evident - one that resonates with your core values and is equally dedicated to amplifying the message you wish to spread. Such communities are not built overnight. They require patience, engagement, and a consistency that assures your audience they are part of something larger than themselves. Finally, the concept of leaving a digital legacy invites us to ponder the mark we wish to leave on the world. It's about leveraging our digital prowess for more than just commercial success or personal fame; it's about initiating a ripple effect of positive change that outlives the ephemeral nature of social media trends. In the grand tapestry of the digital age, those who aspire to create a lasting impact are the ones who understand that at the heart of social media, beyond the algorithms and growth hacks, lies the potential to uplift, inspire, and transform the world, one post at a time.

Inspiring Positive Change Through Social Media

Social media has matured from a simple communication platform into a powerful vehicle for positive change. The scope of influence you wield on these platforms is nothing short of remarkable, allowing not just for virality but for real, tangible impact on the world. Within this transformative space, the potential to inspire shifts in thinking, mobilize communities, and ignite movements is at your fingertips.

Firstly, let's talk about how the essence of your message matters. Every post shared, every story told contributes to a larger narrative. Crafting content that not only draws attention but sparks thought and discussion is crucial. It's about more than just engagement metrics; it's about instigating conversations that matter. Whether it's climate change, mental health awareness, or social equality, your platform can serve as a catalyst for bringing these pivotal subjects to the fore.

Authenticity here is key. The digital audience is savvy, able to discern genuine passion from opportunistic bandwagoning. Therefore, it's vital to champion causes near to your heart. When your followers see your true dedication, they are far more likely to engage deeply with your content and the causes you support. This genuine connection is what transforms passive viewers into active participants in your mission for change.

Collaboration has immense power. Teaming up with like-minded influencers, brands, and non-profits can amplify your message far beyond your current reach. These partnerships not only pool resources but also meld diverse audiences into a unified force for good. Think of it as a multiplier effect, where the sum impact is greater than its parts, driving both awareness and action on an exponentially larger scale.

Creating interactive content plays a significant role as well. From informative polls to thought-provoking challenges, engaging your audience actively not only boosts visibility but also empowers followers to contribute their voice to the cause. This can transform passive consumption into active participation, elevating the level of engagement and investment in the advocated issues.

Moreover, consistency is crucial in keeping the momentum. Initiatives for change are not one-off campaigns but ongoing conversations. Regular updates, stories of progress, and acknowledgments of collective efforts keep the community engaged and motivated. It's about creating a narrative of continuous impact, where each update fuels further interest and action.

Leveraging visual content amplifies this effect. Images and videos can communicate complex messages quickly and emotively, breaking down barriers of language and literacy. They can humanize abstract issues, making them relatable and compelling. A well-constructed visual narrative can stir emotions, driving engagement and sharing, thus spreading the message virally.

Empowering your followers to contribute content can also expand your reach and impact. User-generated content not only provides fresh perspectives but also strengthens the community bond. Encouraging followers to share their stories and experiences related to your cause can foster a sense of belonging, making them feel part of something larger than themselves.

Data can be a powerful storytelling tool as well. Utilizing analytics to understand what resonates with your audience can help tailor your strategy to maximize impact. Choosing the right metrics to focus on, beyond likes and shares, to gauge real-world influence is essential. This helps in refining your approach, ensuring that your efforts are as effective as they can be.

Educational content is another cornerstone of inspiring change. Informing your audience about the issues at hand, providing actionable insights, and debunking myths elevates the level of discourse. This not only enriches your content mix but also positions you as a thought leader in the space, someone who doesn't just advocate for change but actively leads by example.

Remember, the platform you choose plays a significant role in your strategy. Each social media platform has its nuances and preferred content formats. Tailoring your message to fit these platforms can enhance your outreach. Whether it's short, impactful stories on Instagram, detailed expositions on Facebook, or engaging videos on YouTube, understanding where your message fits best is key.

Hashtags, often overlooked, can be potent tools for virality and awareness. Creating or adopting relevant hashtags can help track the conversation, engage with a broader audience, and create a searchable thread on the topic. This aids in not just spreading the word but also in creating a digital footprint that others can follow and contribute to.

Feedback and engagement from your community should never be underestimated. Actively responding to comments, messages, and posts not only builds a stronger community but also provides valuable insights into your audience's perceptions and needs. This two-way communication enriches the relationship, making your followers feel heard and valued, further cementing their commitment to your shared cause.

Yet, amidst all this, self-care should not be sidelined. Championing for change on social platforms can be emotionally taxing. It's important to recognize the weight of what you're undertaking and ensure that you're taking care of your mental and emotional health. Balancing passion with well-being is vital for sustainable impact.

Last but not least, measuring the impact of your initiatives is crucial. Whether it's through tracking engagement metrics, following up on real-world actions taken, or gathering testimonials, understanding the tangible effects of your efforts helps in highlighting the difference you're making. It also serves as inspiration, both for you and your followers, to continue pushing for change.

In conclusion, inspiring positive change through social media is not only about leveraging your platform for good but doing so in a way that is authentic, engaging, and sustainable. It's about understanding the power you hold and using it responsibly to effect real, positive transformation in the world. Your journey to making an impact starts with the realization that every post, every video, and every story counts. It's up to you to make them matter.

Building a Community With Purpose

Embarking on the journey to build a community with purpose on social media is a daunting yet rewarding endeavor. This venture isn't just about amassing numbers; it's about curating a space where meaningful interaction fosters and thrives. Each member of your community matters and contributes to the overarching goals you've set. This chapter focuses on ways to cultivate such an environment, ensuring your community stands the test of time and changes in social media landscapes.

The foundation of a purpose-driven community lies in clear, shared values. Identifying what your community stands for is crucial. These values are the compass that guides everything from content creation to how interactions are managed within the community. Make sure these are communicated clearly and often, so community members feel aligned and motivated by a common cause.

Understanding the power of engagement is next. Engagement in a purposeful community goes beyond likes and comments. It's about creating opportunities for your audience to interact with the content, the brand, and each other in meaningful ways. Ask questions that prompt thought and discussion, create polls to gather opinions, and encourage members to share their stories and experiences that resonate with the community's values.

Transparency is your ally in building trust within your community. Be open about your goals, challenges, and successes. Let your community see the people behind the brand. This doesn't mean over-sharing but choosing moments to peel back the curtain and let your audience in. Trust is built on consistency and honesty, so prioritize these in your interactions.

Creating a sense of belonging is paramount. Each member should feel valued and understood. Highlight community members, celebrate their achievements, and make it known that their contributions are appreciated. Small gestures can have a big impact on making people feel like they're part of something special.

Consistent communication is key. Whether through regular posts, updates, or Q&A sessions, keeping in touch with your community helps maintain engagement levels. Use a tone and style that's relatable and in line with your community's vibe. Consistency in your communication frequency and style reinforces community identity.

Offer value beyond what's expected. Providing exclusive content, insights, or opportunities makes membership in your community uniquely advantageous. This could be through educational content, inspirational posts, or first looks at new products or services.

Encourage member-to-member interaction. Fostering a network where community members can support and learn from each other enriches the community experience. Create spaces or segments within your platform where these interactions can happen organically.

Moderation is necessary to maintain the integrity of your community. Setting clear guidelines on conduct within the community and enforcing these rules ensures that the environment remains respectful and conducive to its intended purpose. This includes being vigilant against hate speech, spam, or any forms of harassment.

Leverage data and feedback to evolve. Listening to your community involved observing both the qualitative and quantitative data. Surveys, feedback forms, and analytics can all provide insights into what's working and what isn't, allowing you to adapt your strategy in meaningful ways.

Celebrate milestones with your community. Whether it's the anniversary of the community, reaching a member count goal, or achieving a collective aim, celebrating these moments strengthens the bond within the community. These celebrations can be virtual events, special content, or community shout-outs.

Collaboration instead of competition should be the ethos your community embraces. Highlighting and collaborating with other communities or influencers that share your values not only broadens your reach but also adds value to your members by bringing diverse perspectives and content.

Plan regular audits of your community strategy. As social media landscapes change, so should your approach to community building. Regularly review your tactics, the platforms you use, and how your community's needs may be evolving. Stay flexible and be prepared to pivot where necessary.

Creating a purpose-driven social media community is not an overnight project. It's a commitment to grow alongside your members, offering them a platform where they feel valued and understood. Your community is a reflection of its members, and as such, it has the potential to be a powerful force for change, connection, and impact.

Remember, the goal isn't just to create a community but to nurture a space where real, meaningful interactions can take place. It's about more than just numbers; it's about creating a sense of belonging, shared purpose, and mutual growth. By focusing on these elements, you're not just building a community; you're fostering a movement.

In the end, the success of your purpose-driven community hinges on your ability to empathize, adapt, and stay true to the values that brought your community together in the first place. With patience, dedication, and strategic actions, your community can become a lasting source of impact and fulfillment both for you and your members.

Leaving a Digital Legacy

In today's fast-paced digital world, leaving a mark that transcends the immediate buzz of the latest viral trend takes more than just momentary fame. It's about creating a digital legacy, a lasting impact that continues to inspire and influence long after the initial wave of virality fades. This chapter is designed to guide you through the essential steps to not only capture the spotlight but also to ensure your presence on social media platforms has a lasting, positive effect on your audience and beyond.

First and foremost, understanding the power of impactful content is crucial. Viral content often captures attention for its humor, shock value, or timeliness, but content that leaves a legacy does more; it resonates on a personal level, offers value, and fosters a deep connection with the audience. To achieve this, focus on the core message you want to be remembered for. This could be anything from inspiring creativity, advocating for social change, or sharing knowledge in a specific niche. Once you've defined your core message, integrate it consistently into your content, making your social media presence a reflection of the legacy you wish to leave.

Transparency and authenticity play a significant role in solidifying your digital legacy. In a sea of curated personas, genuine voices stand out. Share your journey, including the setbacks, learnings, and victories. This honesty not only humanizes you but also builds trust with your audience, making your social media platform a source of inspiration and encouragement.

Engaging actively with your community is another crucial aspect. Legacy is not just about the content you produce but also about the relationships you build and the discussions you spark. Encourage your followers to share their thoughts, stories, and experiences. This two-way interaction amplifies your impact, creating a community that's engaged, loyal, and supportive.

Innovating and staying ahead of trends while steadfastly delivering your core message is a delicate balance but essential for sustaining your influence. As you adapt to new platforms, technologies, and content formats, keep your fundamental values and messages consistent. This adaptability shows your commitment to evolving with your audience while staying true to what you stand for.

Collaborating with other influencers and brands that share your values can amplify your reach and strengthen your legacy. These partnerships allow you to tap into new audiences, offer different perspectives, and reinforce your message through collective efforts.

Another step towards leaving a lasting digital legacy is investing in the education and empowerment of your audience. Whether through tutorials, workshops, or discussions, empowering your followers with skills, knowledge, and confidence ensures your impact goes beyond mere entertainment, transforming your legacy into a force for growth and change.

Consistency is key. While trends come and go, your presence should be constant. A routine posting schedule, regular engagement, and a steadfast adherence to your values assure your audience that you're a reliable figure in the ever-changing digital landscape.

Finally, plan for the future. Think about how your digital assets can continue to inspire, educate, and entertain, even when you're not actively managing them. From creating timeless content that will remain relevant for years to come to setting up systems that allow your platforms to continue to function and evolve, planning for permanence ensures that your digital legacy will endure.

To leave a digital legacy, you must think beyond the horizon of immediate gains and fleeting fame. It's about cultivating an ecosystem where content lives, values thrive, and communities grow. By focusing on your core message, building genuine connections, and continuously evolving, your digital presence can leave an indelible mark on the world, ensuring your influence lasts for generations to come.

Chapter 15:
Advanced Monetization Techniques

After honing the art of capturing attention on social media, the next crucial step is turning that engagement into a steady revenue stream. It's all about leveraging the platform beyond the basics to create income. Advanced monetization requires a toolkit that extends your reach and deepens your connection with your audience. Consider this: every follower is a potential customer. That's where the power of email marketing comes into play, allowing you not only to reach out directly but also to personalize your communication. This approach not only drives sales but also builds a deeper relationship with your audience.

Creating and selling digital products offers an unparalleled opportunity to monetize your expertise or creativity. Whether it's an ebook, online course, or exclusive video content, digital products can provide a significant income with the right strategy. It's essential to create offerings that resonate with your audience's needs and desires. By doing so, you provide value that they're more than willing to pay for.

Lastly, social media advertising should not be overlooked. With advanced targeting options, you can reach potential buyers outside of your current following. This is not just about spreading the word; it's about spreading it to the right people. Investing in ads can seem daunting at first, but with a focus on ROI and a keen eye on analytics, you can turn a modest ad spend into a significant return. Remember, it's about smart spending, targeting your ads for maximum impact, and constantly refining your approach based on performance data. Utilizing these advanced monetization techniques, you can transform your social media platforms from mere showcases of content into dynamic, revenue-generating engines.

Leveraging Email Marketing

In the realm of advanced monetization techniques, email marketing emerges as a sterling strategy that, if executed correctly, can significantly amplify your brand's revenue stream. While the allure of social media platforms is undeniable, the power of a well-crafted email shouldn't be underestimated. This section aims to peel back the layers of email marketing, offering actionable insights on how it can be intertwined with your social media efforts to create a robust monetization framework.

Firstly, understanding the symbiosis between social media and email marketing is crucial. While social media excels at capturing attention and building community, email marketing excels at driving conversions. By engaging your social media audience and then funneling them into a well-segmented email list, you create an opportunity to speak to them directly, in a space that is uniquely personal: their inbox.

Creating a seamless bridge from your social media platforms to your email list is quintessential. Tactics such as exclusive email sign-up bonuses, previews of email content on your social channels, or even running social media contests that require email sign-up can effectively grow your list. Remember, the aim is to offer value so compelling that your audience can't help but want to be a part of your email community.

Segmentation is the secret weapon of email marketing. Not all followers are created equal; their interests can vary widely. By segmenting your email list based on behavior, engagement, or demographics, you tailor your messages so they resonate deeply with each subset of your audience. This personalization enhances the likelihood of conversions, as messages feel more relevant and less like broad strokes.

Content, as in all forms of digital marketing, holds the throne in email marketing too. Your email content should be engaging, informative, and, most importantly, in alignment with the expectations set when they signed up. Whether it's insider tips, the latest industry news, exclusive offers, or personal stories, consistent delivery of quality content will keep your audience engaged and less likely to hit the unsubscribe button.

Integrating social proof into your emails can significantly bolster your credibility. Highlight user-generated content, customer testimonials, or notable mentions of your brand. This not only showcases your community's enthusiasm for your brand but also leverages the psychological principle of social proof, encouraging more engagement and investment in your offerings.

Call-to-actions (CTAs) in emails should not be an afterthought. Each email should have a clear goal, accompanied by a CTA that guides the reader to the next step. Whether it's visiting a landing page, taking advantage of a sale, or following you on a new social media platform, CTAs transform passive reading into actionable engagement.

Testing and optimization are key to refining your email marketing strategy. A/B testing subject lines, email layouts, or CTAs can provide valuable insights into what resonates best with your audience. Coupled with a keen eye on analytics like open rates, click-through rates, and conversion rates, these tests can significantly improve the effectiveness of your campaigns.

Automation and scalability need to be part of your email marketing strategy from the get-go. Tools that allow for the automation of welcome emails, follow-ups, and even personalized birthday messages can provide a consistent touchpoint with your audience, saving time while enhancing the personal connection with your brand.

Privacy and compliance cannot be overlooked. With regulations like GDPR in the EU and CAN-SPAM in the US, ensuring your email marketing practices are compliant is not just good practice, it's a necessity. This includes obtaining explicit consent to email individuals and providing clear, easy options to unsubscribe. Respecting your audience's privacy is non-negotiable for long-term trust and retention.

Leverage the analytics offered by your email marketing platform. Understanding your audience's behavior — not just who they are, but how they interact with your emails — informs adjustments to your strategy. If certain types of content consistently yield higher engagement, pivot to include more of that content. If particular segments are less responsive, consider re-engagement campaigns or further segmentation for more targeted communication.

Integration with other marketing tools and platforms can magnify your email marketing efforts. For instance, connecting your email marketing software with your CRM can provide a more detailed picture of your customer journey, from the initial social media touchpoint through to email engagement and, ultimately, conversion.

Email marketing, when done well, can directly impact your bottom line. By viewing it as a long-term strategy rather than a quick fix, it's possible to cultivate a deeply engaged list of subscribers who are more likely to convert into paying customers. Remember, acquiring a new customer is often more costly than retaining an existing one, making your email list an invaluable asset.

Finally, never underestimate the power of a strong narrative. Just like in social media, storytelling in emails can captivate your audience, making your brand memorable and your messages eagerly anticipated. Crafting emails that are not only informative but also entertaining and relatable can significantly strengthen your audience's loyalty and advocacy for your brand.

In conclusion, leveraging email marketing as part of a comprehensive social media strategy is not merely advantageous; it's essential. By treating email marketing with the same creativity, strategic planning, and analytical rigour as your social media endeavors, you're not just reaching your audience. You're engaging them in a meaningful dialogue that can lead to sustained growth, loyalty, and profitability. As social media platforms continue to evolve, your email list stands as a constant — a direct line to your most engaged fans that, if nurtured correctly, will pay dividends for years to come.

Creating and Selling Digital Products

Now that you've mastered the art of building a vibrant social media presence, it's time to level up your game with advanced monetization techniques. One powerful strategy is creating and selling digital products. This approach not only provides a tangible value to your followers but also establishes a steady income stream for you. Let's dive into how to conceptualize, create, and market digital products effectively.

The first step is identifying what kind of digital product to create. This decision should be rooted in your expertise, audience interest, and market demand. E-books, online courses, exclusive videos, templates, or even software tools can become your product offering. Understanding your audience's challenges and how you can solve them will guide your product development.

Creating a digital product requires a structured plan. Begin with outlining your product content, format, and delivery method. For online courses, break down the syllabus into manageable sections. If you're creating an e-book, map out chapters that provide progressive value to the reader. This phase is about structuring your knowledge into a cohesive, saleable product.

Quality content is key. Your digital product should not only resonate with your audience but also exceed their expectations. Investing time in content creation, be it writing, filming, or designing, ensures your product's value. High-quality, actionable content will help build trust and credibility with your audience, encouraging them to invest.

Branding your product is just as important as its content. Your product's visual and narrative branding should align with your overall social media presence for consistency. A strong brand identity for your product makes it easily recognizable and amplifies its appeal. Don't forget to give your product a catchy, self-explanatory name.

The platform you choose to sell your digital products on plays a crucial role in their success. Whether you opt for a personal website, a dedicated marketplace, or even through social media platforms directly, ensure that the chosen platform supports your needs and reaches your target audience effectively.

Setting the right price for your product can be tricky but is crucial. Research competitors, understand your audience's purchasing power, and consider the perceived value of your product. It's often recommended to offer multiple pricing tiers or bundles to cater to different segments of your audience.

Launching your digital product involves strategic planning. Leveraging your social media platforms, tease your audience with sneak peeks, behind-the-scenes content, and exclusive offers. Creating a launch event or a countdown can generate excitement and anticipation.

Marketing your digital product should leverage both organic and paid strategies. Use social media posts, stories, and ads to reach a wider audience. Email marketing can also be a powerful tool to engage potential buyers, providing them with valuable insights and exclusive deals.

User testimonials and reviews can significantly impact your digital product's credibility. Encourage early buyers to give feedback and showcase these testimonials prominently. Social proof can be a decisive factor for potential buyers on the fence.

To keep the momentum going post-launch, continuously engage with your audience about your product. Share success stories, additional tips related to your product's content, and updates or expansions to your product line. Keeping the conversation going can lead to repeat business and new buyers.

Scaling your digital product business could involve creating a series of products or complementary products that satisfy the broader needs and interests of your audience. Analyze the performance of your initial products to identify opportunities for expansion or improvement.

Legal considerations, such as copyright and licensing issues, should not be overlooked. Ensure that your digital products comply with relevant laws and regulations. Protecting your intellectual property while respecting others' rights is paramount.

Feedback and data analysis are vital for improving your product and strategy. Monitor sales data, collect customer feedback, and adjust your marketing and product development efforts based on insights gained. This iterative process ensures that your offerings remain relevant and desired.

Finally, it's essential to stay updated on trends not just in your niche, but also in digital product creation and marketing at large. Innovations in technology, changes in customer behavior, and new marketing platforms can offer opportunities to grow your digital product business further.

In conclusion, creating and selling digital products is a profound way to monetize your social media presence. It requires understanding your audience, creating valuable content, effective branding and marketing, and continuous engagement and improvement. With dedication and strategic planning, your digital products can become a significant source of income and impact.

Investing in Social Media Advertising

In the current landscape of digital marketing, investing in social media advertising stands as a non-negotiable element for anyone aiming to escalate their online presence significantly. This chapter takes you through the ins and outs of making the most out of your advertising dollars on various social media platforms. It's all about optimizing for the highest return on investment (ROI) while navigating through the complexities of targeted advertising.

Firstly, it's vital to understand the unique advantages that social media advertising offers. Unlike traditional marketing channels, social media platforms provide the ability to pinpoint your target audience with remarkable accuracy. This precision ensures that your advertisements reach the eyeballs of those who are most likely to engage with your content, follow your profiles, and, eventually, convert into loyal customers or fans.

Before diving into the specifics of crafting your ad campaigns, let's talk budgeting. Determining how much to spend on social media ads is more art than science. Start with a budget you're comfortable with and refine as you go, based on the performance analytics provided by platforms. The key is to start small, test continuously, and scale your spend based on what works. Remember, even a modest budget can yield substantial results if allocated wisely.

Creating compelling ads that resonate with your target audience is next on the agenda. This calls for a deep dive into understanding who your followers are and what they care about. Utilize the demographic and psychographic segmentation tools offered by social media platforms to tailor your messages accordingly. Personalization is paramount; an ad that feels personal and relevant is far more likely to captivate and convert.

The choice of format for your advertisement is another critical decision. From images and videos to carousels and stories, each format serves different purposes and excels under various circumstances. For instance, video ads are typically more engaging and have higher conversion rates for products that require demonstrations. However, the right choice depends heavily on your specific objectives and the nature of your content.

A/B testing, or split testing, is an indispensable technique in optimizing your social media advertising efforts. By creating two versions of your ad and tweaking one single element, you can compare their performance to see which version resonates more with your audience. This iterative process leads to better engagement rates and a higher ROI over time, as you continuously refine your approach based on empirical evidence.

Investing in influencer partnerships as a component of your advertising strategy can amplify your reach exponentially. Influencers with a loyal following can introduce your brand or content to a wider audience in a more organic and trustworthy manner. The key is to choose influencers whose followers overlap significantly with your target audience.

Measuring the success of your social media ads isn't solely about tracking likes and shares. Delve deeper into analytics to understand metrics like click-through rates (CTR), conversion rates, and cost per acquisition (CPA). These metrics provide a clearer picture of how effectively your ad spend converts into tangible outcomes such as sales, sign-ups, or other conversion goals.

Riding the wave of emerging trends and leveraging them in your advertisements can set you apart from the competition. Whether it's incorporating augmented reality experiences or tapping into meme culture, staying ahead of the curve can make your ads more engaging and share-worthy.

Privacy and ethical considerations in social media advertising cannot be overstated. With increasing scrutiny on data usage and privacy concerns, it's necessary to be transparent about how you collect and use data. Ensuring compliance with regulations like GDPR and maintaining ethical standards in your ads not only fosters trust with your audience but also safeguards your brand's reputation.

Localization of your ads is crucial if you're targeting a global audience. Customizing your advertisements to fit the linguistic and cultural nuances of different regions can drastically improve their effectiveness. This might mean more than just translating the text; it might also involve adapting visuals and messaging to resonate better with diverse audiences.

Retargeting is a powerful strategy in social media advertising that enables you to reach people who have previously interacted with your brand. Whether they visited your website, liked a post, or added a product to their cart without purchasing, retargeting ads serve as reminders and prompts, significantly increasing the chances of conversion.

Finally, monitoring and adapting to the ever-changing algorithms of social media platforms is crucial. Platforms frequently update their algorithms, which can dramatically affect the visibility and performance of your ads. Staying informed and being willing to adjust your strategy accordingly is essential for sustained success.

To summarize, investing in social media advertising is a multifaceted endeavor that requires a strategic approach. From budgeting and targeting to format selection and analytics, every decision plays a critical role in determining the ROI of your advertising campaigns. By continuously testing, learning, and adapting, you can leverage the immense power of social media advertising to grow your presence, engage your audience, and achieve your monetization goals.

Remember, while the landscape of social media is ever-evolving, the core principle remains the same: connect with your audience in meaningful ways. Social media advertising, when done right, is not just about selling a product or service—it's about building relationships. With the right strategy, you can not only capture attention but also win hearts, turning followers into fans and customers into advocates.

Chapter 16:
Maximizing International Reach

Expanding your social media reach beyond your home country's borders isn't just about translating your content into different languages; it's about truly understanding and engaging with diverse cultures and global trends. To truly maximize your international reach, you've got to dive deep into cultural nuances. This means creating content that resonates on a local level in various global markets, which might involve collaborating with local influencers or using region-specific hashtags. It's also about identifying global trends early and adapting them in a way that's authentic to your brand and engaging for an international audience. Language is just the beginning; adapting your strategy to include culturally relevant content can transform your social media channels into global platforms. Tools and analytics can provide insights into which countries are engaging with your content, enabling you to tailor your approach further and refine your strategy over time. The goal isn't just to be seen across the globe but to connect and resonate with international audiences in a way that feels personal and meaningful. By doing so, you're not just broadening your reach; you're building a truly global community.

Overcoming Language Barriers

As we pivot to maximizing our reach across international boundaries, we inevitably encounter the challenge of language barriers. This divide can seem daunting but isn't insurmountable. With strategic planning and implementation of specific tactics, you can bridge the gap, connect with a global audience, and truly make your mark on the world stage of social media.

First, it's essential to recognize the power of translation tools and services. While automatic translations aren't always perfect, they've come a long way. Leveraging these can help make your content more accessible to non-English speakers. However, for content that's crucial to your brand's message, consider investing in professional translation services to ensure accuracy and cultural sensitivity.

Another key strategy is to produce content in English but include subtitles or captions in multiple languages. This is particularly effective for video content on platforms like YouTube or Instagram. There's a wealth of tools available that can help you add subtitles efficiently, ensuring your message gets across loud and clear, regardless of your viewers' primary language.

Speaking of clarity, simplifying your content can also help bridge the language gap. Complex idioms, puns, and culturally specific references might not translate well. Aim for straightforward, universally understandable content that resonates with a wide audience. This doesn't mean dumbing down your content but rather making it more accessible.

Engagement doesn't just have to be about the content you're creating; it can also be about how you interact with your audience. Responding to comments, messages, and engaging in conversations using simple, clear language can foster a stronger connection with your international audience. Even using a basic understanding of another language or a polite greeting can go a long way.

Consider the role of global influencers and communities in your strategy. Collaborating with influencers who speak different languages or hail from various countries can provide an authentic way to connect with new audiences. They can also offer valuable insights into cultural nuances that you might miss.

It's also worthwhile to look into creating different profiles for different geographical or linguistic markets. While this might increase your workload, having a dedicated profile for a specific language or country allows you to tailor your content more precisely to different segments of your global audience.

Don't forget about the visual aspects of your content. Images, videos, and infographics that rely more on visuals than on text can transcend language barriers. Ensure that the visuals you use are culturally appropriate and universally appealing to maximize their impact.

Machine learning and artificial intelligence have made leaps and bounds in the area of language translation and content personalization. Utilize these technologies to your advantage. Many social media platforms offer automatic translation features for posts and comments. Explore these options to make your content more accessible.

User-generated content can also be a powerful tool in overcoming language barriers. Encourage your followers to share their own stories, photos, and videos related to your brand or campaigns. This not only boosts engagement but also provides content in a variety of languages, making your brand more relatable to a global audience.

When it comes to written content, consider the layout and design. Ensure that the text is easy to read and that your website or social media profile supports different scripts used in other languages. This technical aspect is crucial for truly inclusive and accessible content.

Localization goes beyond mere translation. It involves adapting your content to suit the cultural context and preferences of your target audience. This can mean changing visuals, modifying messaging, or even altering your product offerings based on cultural sensibilities.

Engaging with a diverse set of beta testers or focus groups from around the world can provide invaluable feedback on how your content is perceived across different languages and cultures. This feedback can guide adjustments to make your content more universally appealing.

Always be learning. The global digital landscape is constantly evolving, so stay informed about the latest trends in global content creation and linguistic technology. This proactive approach will help you adapt quickly and keep your international engagement strategies effective.

Lastly, cultivate patience and a willingness to learn from mistakes. Overcoming language barriers in social media isn't just about expanding your reach; it's about building genuine connections and understanding across cultures. It's a gradual process that requires time, effort, and an open mind.

In conclusion, breaking down language barriers is a multifaceted challenge that rewards those willing to put in the effort with a truly global audience. By leveraging technology, simplifying and localizing content, and embracing cultural diversity, you can extend your social media empire's reach far beyond your initial expectations. It's a journey of continuous learning and adaptation, but one that opens up a world of possibilities for growth and engagement.

Cultural Considerations in Content Creation

Capturing the attention of a global audience means understanding and respecting the diverse tapestry of cultures that make up this audience. Creating content that resonates across borders requires a sensitivity to cultural nuances that can either forge connections or create divides. Let's dive into the myriad of considerations one must juggle to achieve international acclaim.

First and foremost, it's imperative to conduct thorough research into the cultural norms and values of the regions you're targeting. What's considered humorous, inspiring, or relatable can vary wildly from culture to culture. An innocent gesture or phrase in one country can carry a negative connotation in another. Hence, a nuanced approach toward understanding these differences is the first step in creating content that is universally appealing.

Localization doesn't just stop at translating language; it extends to adapting your content to reflect local customs, traditions, and holidays. Celebrating International Women's Day might be customary in many parts of the world, but how each culture observes this day can provide unique opportunities for targeted content that resonates on a personal level.

Diversity in your content is another key element. Featuring a range of cultures, languages, and settings in your visuals and narratives not only broadens your appeal but also helps in building a global brand identity that is inclusive. Representation matters, and audiences are more likely to engage with content that reflects a world they recognize.

Understanding localized social media trends and challenges is crucial. While some trends might be global, many rise from regional preferences and viral moments. Tapping into these localized trends can significantly enhance your content's relevance and shareability.

Be mindful of cultural sensitivities and avoid stereotypes. Generalizations can quickly lead to misinterpretation and backlash. Aim for authenticity by engaging with and learning from the communities you wish to represent. This respect for cultural authenticity will earn you credibility and trust among international audiences.

Consider the role of religion, as it plays a significant and sensitive role in many cultures. Content that aligns or conflicts with religious beliefs can deeply affect its reception. Being aware of religious holidays, practices, and taboos can inform your content calendar and strategy, avoiding potential pitfalls.

Also, remember that humor doesn't always translate. What's funny in one culture may be lost or, worse, offensive in another. If humor is a part of your brand's voice, seek advice from cultural consultants to ensure it crosses cultural boundaries gracefully.

Prioritize visual storytelling, which can often cross linguistic and cultural barriers more effectively than text. However, even visuals require cultural consideration—colors, gestures, and symbols can have vastly different meanings across the world.

Engagement practices may also vary between cultures. Strategies to encourage comments, shares, and likes in one country might not work in another. Understanding these nuances can help tailor your calls-to-action and engagement techniques to suit diverse audiences.

It's equally important to be aware of global issues and how different cultures perceive them. Showing sensitivity and support for issues that matter worldwide can not only boost your content's relevance but also showcase your brand as socially responsible.

Adapting your content's format to suit the preferred platforms of your target regions can also impact your reach. Some countries may favour certain social media platforms over others. Tailoring your content to fit the dominant platforms in your target regions can improve visibility and engagement.

Feedback is a precious resource when navigating cultural nuances. Regularly engage with your international audience to gather insights and understand their perspective. This direct feedback can guide content adjustments and foster a sense of community and belonging among your viewers.

In conclusion, when content creators embrace and respect cultural differences, they unlock the potential to reach and resonate with a truly global audience. As you venture into international waters with your content, let empathy, respect, and inclusivity be your guiding stars. This approach not only maximizes your reach but enriches your content with the beauty of diversity, paving the way for authentic connections and lasting engagements across the globe.

Last but not least, always be willing to learn, adapt, and improve. The global cultural landscape is continually evolving, and staying informed is key to maintaining relevance and resonance in your content creation journey. Your ability to navigate cultural considerations effectively is a powerful tool in maximizing your international reach, bringing you closer to achieving viral success on a global scale.

Utilizing Global Trends for Local Success

In the vast world of social media, understanding and leveraging global trends can amplify your reach and strengthen your brand's footprint. But the real magic happens when you can harness these trends and make them resonate with your local audience. This chapter delves into the intricacies of turning global phenomena into local victories.

Firstly, it's essential to keep a keen eye on the pulse of global movements within your niche. Social media platforms provide a treasure trove of insights into what's trending worldwide. But the key isn't just to replicate these trends; it's about adding your unique twist that speaks directly to your local community.

For instance, if a particular challenge goes viral globally, think about how you can adapt it to reflect local flavors or issues. This could mean incorporating local dialects, landscapes, or culturally relevant themes. Remember, the more your audience can see themselves in your content, the more they'll engage.

Understanding local culture and sensitivities is paramount. What works in one region might not resonate, or might even offend, in another. Take the time to research and understand the local context before jumping on a global trend. This approach ensures your content is not just seen, but also appreciated and shared.

Language plays a crucial role in localizing global trends. While English might be the lingua franca of the internet, don't underestimate the power of communicating in your local language. It adds a layer of personalization and shows your commitment to your local audience.

But how do you find these global trends? Regularly monitor platforms like Twitter, TikTok, and Instagram to see what's catching fire. Use tools that track trending hashtags and conversations across these platforms. Once you've identified a trend, brainstorm ways to localize it for your audience.

Collaboration can also play a significant role in this strategy. Partner with local influencers or brands to give the trend a familiar face. These collaborations not only bring authenticity to your content but also expand your reach within the local community.

Don't forget to measure the impact of your localized content. Use analytics tools to track engagement rates, shares, and feedback. This data will provide valuable insights into what resonates with your audience and help refine your future content.

Consider the timing of adopting global trends. Sometimes, being the first to localize a trend can set you apart, but in other instances, waiting to see its global impact can offer insights into how best to adapt it locally. Strategic timing can make all the difference.

Moreover, as you adapt global trends, it's crucial to maintain your brand's voice and integrity. While it's tempting to jump on every viral trend, ensure that each piece of content aligns with your brand's image and values. This consistency is what keeps your audience loyal and engaged.

Another aspect to consider is sustainability. In the rush to adapt to fast-moving trends, it's important to think about the long-term implications of your content. Aim for timeless value that contributes to building your brand, rather than just momentary spikes in attention.

Also, consider leveraging technology to better understand and interpret global trends for your local audience. Artificial intelligence and machine learning tools can provide insights into global content performance and help predict trends likely to capture interest.

In addition, always be prepared to pivot. The digital landscape is ever-changing, and what works today might not tomorrow. Keeping a flexible content strategy allows you to quickly adapt to new trends as they emerge, maintaining your relevance and appeal.

At the heart of utilizing global trends for local success is creativity and authenticity. While it's about tapping into the global zeitgeist, it's equally about celebrating local identity and culture. By carefully balancing these elements, you can create content that's globally informed yet distinctly local.

In conclusion, the art of localizing global trends is a dynamic and rewarding strategy in the quest for social media success. It demands an understanding of both the global digital landscape and the nuances of local culture. With careful planning, creativity, and a finger on the pulse of both global and local currents, you can captivate your audience and set your brand apart in the crowded digital arena.

Chapter 17:
Crafting Viral Campaigns

In this chapter, we delve into the art and science of creating viral campaigns that can catapult your social media presence to new heights. At the heart of a successful viral campaign is understanding the delicate balance between relatability and creativity. It's about tapping into the current zeitgeist or even establishing an entirely new trend. We'll guide you through planning and executing viral challenges that not only capture the imagination of your audience but encourage active participation. You'll learn how to harness the power of memes and internet culture, transforming them into a potent tool in your viral arsenal. Importantly, this chapter addresses the dos and don'ts of viral marketing, offering key insights into navigating this unpredictable yet highly rewarding landscape. Whether it's creating content that effortlessly crosses cultural and linguistic barriers, or ensuring your viral content pushes the envelope without crossing the line, this chapter empowers you with the tools and knowledge necessary to make an indelible mark on the digital world. By the end of this chapter, you'll be equipped with the strategies to not just chase virality but to create campaigns that resonate deeply, driving engagement and fostering a sense of community around your brand or persona.

Planning and Executing Viral Challenges

Viral challenges are an essential part of the playbook for anyone aiming to capture the ever-shifting attention of social media users. They're unpredictable, engaging, and if executed correctly, can propel your social media presence into the stratosphere. Planning them, though, isn't just about throwing ideas at the wall and seeing what sticks; it's an art and science unto itself.

The foundation of a successful viral challenge lies in its relatability and simplicity. The idea should be easy to understand and execute, ensuring that the majority of your audience can participate without needing a tutorial. Think of the ice bucket challenge – its beauty was in its simplicity. You dump a bucket of ice water over your head, challenge others to do the same, and suddenly, you've got a movement that not only goes viral but drives meaningful impact.

Understanding your target audience is crucial when you're planning a viral challenge. Dive into analytics, explore their interests, and identify content that resonates with them. This insight will guide you in tailoring your challenge in a way that not only appeals to them but also encourages engagement and sharing.

Another key aspect is leveraging current trends or topical events. Challenges that tap into the zeitgeist have a higher chance of going viral because they're already part of the larger social conversation. However, timing is everything. Jumping in too late on a trend can make your challenge seem like an afterthought.

When it comes to executing your viral challenge, transparency and clarity are your best friends. Participants should know exactly what to do, how to do it, and why they're doing it. If your challenge supports a cause, make that connection clear. People are more likely to participate if they feel they're contributing to something bigger than themselves.

Creating a unique hashtag for your challenge is non-negotiable. It's not just a way to track participation; it's also a tool for increasing visibility. As the challenge spreads, the hashtag becomes a clickable link to a community of content centered around your initiative.

Engagement is the fuel that propels challenges across the digital landscape. Actively participating, sharing, and commenting on challenge submissions not only boosts the challenge's visibility but also builds community and connection with your audience. Show genuine interest and appreciation for their efforts – it goes a long way.

Collaborations can also elevate your challenge. Partnering with influencers or brands that align with your mission can amplify your reach. However, choose your partners wisely. Their audience should mirror or complement your target demographic to ensure the collaboration is mutually beneficial.

Don't forget to monitor and adapt. Keeping an eye on how your challenge is received and engaging with participants can offer insights into potential tweaks or adjustments. Sometimes, the smallest adjustments can reignite interest and participation mid-way through.

Incentivizing participation can spur interest and action. Whether it's recognition, a prize, or contributing to a cause, giving people a reason to join in can make a significant difference. Ensure that the incentive aligns with your audience's values and interests for maximum impact.

Remember, not every challenge will go viral, and that's okay. The digital landscape is fickle, and what works one day may not the next. Take risks, learn from the outcomes, and use those lessons to refine your approach for the next challenge.

Analyze the data post-challenge. Look at engagement rates, participation levels, and how far your challenge reached. These metrics are invaluable for understanding what worked, what didn't, and why. Use this data to improve future challenges and strategies.

Lastly, always ensure your challenge is inclusive and respectful. In the pursuit of virality, it's easy to overlook how your challenge could be perceived by different communities. Steer clear of content that may be considered insensitive or offensive. The goal is to unite, not divide.

In conclusion, planning and executing a viral challenge requires creativity, understanding your audience, leveraging trends, clear communication, engagement, and a dash of luck. Embrace the process, learn from each campaign, and continuously refine your strategies. Who knows – your next challenge could be the one that captures the world's imagination.

Whether you're looking to grow your follower count, raise awareness for a cause, or simply engage your audience in a fun, meaningful way, viral challenges can be a powerful tool in your social media arsenal. With careful planning, execution, and a little bit of courage to try something new, you're well on your way to creating a buzz that could take your social media presence to new heights.

Leveraging Memes and Internet Culture

In the realm of social media, understanding and utilizing the power of memes and internet culture is like having an ace up your sleeve. Memes, those humorous images or videos that spread virally, are at the heart of internet culture, acting as a universal language that crosses boundaries of geography, language, and even platforms. In this section, we're diving deep into how you can harness the energy of memes and broader internet culture to create campaigns that don't just aspire to go viral—they catch fire and spread with an unstoppable momentum.

First and foremost, it's crucial to appreciate the nuanced ecosystem of memes and internet culture. Memes aren't just about being funny; they're a form of social commentary, a way for people to connect over shared experiences, and a powerful tool for signaling in-group membership. As a content creator looking to go viral, understanding the layers beneath the surface of a popular meme can provide invaluable insights into what captures the imagination and attention of your target audience.

Staying abreast of trending memes is a full-time job in itself. Platforms like Reddit, Twitter, and TikTok offer a real-time pulse on what's capturing the internet's attention at any given moment. But just because a meme is popular doesn't mean it's right for your brand or campaign. The key is to find or create memes that resonate with your brand's voice and your audience's values. When done right, a well-timed meme that aligns with your message can significantly amplify your campaign's reach and engagement.

One common pitfall in leveraging memes is the temptation to jump on every trend. The internet's users are savvy; they can smell insincerity from a mile away. Your use of memes should feel natural and authentic. It's better to pass on a trend than to force a meme that doesn't fit with your brand, as this can alienate your audience and dilute your message.

Creating original memes related to your niche is another strategy that can yield dividends. This requires creativity and a deep understanding of both your audience and the mechanics of viral content. Original memes that hit the mark can not only go viral themselves but also serve to reinforce your brand's identity and message in a crowded marketplace.

Collaborating with meme creators and influencers is a tactic that should not be overlooked. These individuals are the pulse of what's funny and relevant online; their endorsement or involvement in your campaign can lend authenticity and significantly extend its reach. When selecting collaborators, look for alignment in audience demographics and values to ensure the partnership feels cohesive and genuine.

Timing, as in much of life, is everything when it comes to memes. The lifecycle of a meme can be incredibly short-lived. Striking while the iron is hot is essential to capitalizing on a trend, but so is knowing when a meme has run its course. Posting a meme after its expiration date can make your brand seem out of touch.

Customizing memes for different platforms is also key. What works on Twitter may not necessarily resonate with Instagram's audience, and vice versa. Tailoring your meme to fit the context and norms of each platform can improve its performance and impact.

Metrics and testing should guide your meme strategy. Like any other content, analyzing how memes perform on your channels can provide insights into what works and what doesn't. Use this data to refine your approach, experimenting with different types of memes, posting times, and formats to continuously improve your results.

But it's not all about laughter and likes. Memes can also be a vehicle for sparking conversations and building community. Engaging with followers in the comments of meme posts, asking for their input, or encouraging them to create their own versions can foster an interactive and lively online community.

Legal considerations shouldn't be overlooked. While most memes fall under fair use, ensuring that you have the right to use an image, video, or piece of music is crucial to avoiding copyright issues. Additionally, be mindful of respect and ethics; steer clear of memes that could be considered offensive or alienate parts of your audience.

Ultimately, the goal is to seamlessly integrate memes and internet culture into your broader social media strategy. They should complement your other content, not overshadow it. Memes are a tool in your arsenal, potent for their ability to humanize your brand, make it relevant, and significantly extend your reach.

As we wrap up this section, remember that leveraging memes and internet culture for viral campaigns is both an art and a science. It requires staying informed, being creative, respecting your audience, and sometimes, taking a calculated risk. With the right approach, memes can elevate your social media presence, endearing your brand to a wider audience and driving unprecedented engagement.

So, as you craft your next viral campaign, consider how you can incorporate memes and elements of internet culture not just to ride the wave of current trends, but to connect with your audience in a meaningful, memorable way. It's an ongoing journey of learning and adaptation, but one that can yield significant rewards in the digital landscape.

The landscape of memes and internet culture is ever-evolving, and keeping your finger on the pulse of this dynamic world can ensure that your campaigns stay fresh, relevant, and poised for virality. In the next chapters, we'll explore more strategies to keep your content engaging and your growth strategies adaptable. But never underestimate the power of a well-placed meme to transform your social media presence from mere background noise to a resounding echo across the digital sphere.

The Dos and Don'ts of Viral Marketing

In crafting successful viral campaigns, there's a thin line between epic success and a cringe-worthy flop. Viral marketing, when done right, can catapult your brand into the spotlight, but it requires a delicate balance of creativity, timing, and understanding of your audience. Let's dive into some essential dos and don'ts that can make or break your viral marketing efforts.

Do understand your audience deeply. Before you launch any campaign with the hope of going viral, you need to know who you're talking to. What resonates with them? What are their pain points, interests, and desires? Tailoring your content to match the preferences and values of your audience increases the likelihood of it being shared.

Don't ignore the importance of timing. Cultural moments, trending topics, and current events can serve as a launching pad for viral content. However, you must be swift and sensitive in your response. Jumping on a trend too late or mishandling a sensitive topic can do more harm than good.

Do focus on creating value. Whether it's entertainment, inspiration, or information, your content needs to add value to the lives of your audience. People share content that they find useful or that they think will add value to others. Before hitting publish, ask yourself, "What will my audience gain from this?"

Don't try too hard to sell. Overtly promotional messages disguised as viral attempts often fall flat. The goal of a viral marketing campaign is first and foremost to engage and entertain. Sales and promotional messages should be secondary and subtle, or you risk alienating your audience.

Do make sharing easy. If your content is difficult to share, you're putting a barrier in the path of virality. Ensure your sharing buttons are visible and functional. Encourage sharing by asking for it in your content or through compelling calls to action.

Don't overlook the power of visuals. In today's digital world, visuals are king. Photos, videos, infographics, and memes are more likely to be shared than text-only content. Investing time in creating high-quality, eye-catching visuals can pay off in your campaign's shareability.

Do leverage emotions. Content that elicits strong emotional reactions, whether it's joy, surprise, or even anger, is more likely to be shared. Think about how you can connect with your audience on an emotional level to boost engagement and sharing.

Don't neglect the importance of a good hook. In an age of short attention spans, your content needs to grab attention from the get-go. Work on crafting an irresistible headline or opening that compels people to watch, read, or listen further.

Do encourage participation. Viral campaigns often have an element of participation or interaction. From hashtag challenges to user-generated content campaigns, find ways to involve your audience in the narrative. This not only increases engagement but also investment in the spread of the campaign.

Don't forget to analyze and adjust. Not every attempt at virality will be a home run. It's crucial to continually analyze the performance of your campaigns, understand what worked and what didn't, and adjust your strategy accordingly. Learning from both successes and failures is key to refining your viral marketing efforts.

Do remember the platform. Each social media platform has its own language and norms. What works on Twitter might not resonate on TikTok. Tailor your content and its presentation to fit the platform you're targeting for the best chance of going viral.

Don't underestimate the effort. Going viral might seem like it happens overnight, but behind every successful viral campaign is a lot of strategic planning and effort. Be prepared to invest time in research, content creation, and engagement to truly make an impact.

Do maintain authenticity. In the quest to go viral, don't lose sight of your brand's voice and values. Authenticity resonates with audiences, building trust and loyalty beyond the viral moment. Stay true to your brand, and your audience will be more likely to stick with you for the long haul.

Don't ignore the legal and ethical aspects. In a bid to create engaging content, don't overlook copyright laws, permissions, and ethical considerations. Respecting intellectual property and depicting individuals or situations ethically is paramount to maintaining your brand's integrity.

In conclusion, while there's no surefire formula for virality, adhering to these dos and don'ts can significantly increase your chances. It's about striking the right balance between creativity, strategy, and understanding of your audience. With persistence and a keen eye for what makes content shareable, your next campaign might just be the one to go viral.

Chapter 18:
Developing a Mobile-First Strategy

In today's warp-speed digital landscape, creating content that resonates with mobile users isn't just an option—it's a necessity. Recognizing the dominion of smartphones in our daily lives, a mobile-first approach has emerged as the cornerstone of a successful digital strategy. This chapter delves into optimizing your content for mobile consumption, emphasizing the importance of speed, simplicity, and the capability to engage audiences who are perpetually on the move. It's crucial to acknowledge that the user experience on mobile vastly differs from that on desktop. From the size of your content to the speed at which your page loads, every detail counts towards keeping your audience engaged. Mobile users crave content that is not only easily accessible but also swift and straightforward to consume. By focusing on these aspects, you're not just adapting to the present; you're gearing up for a future wherein mobile continues to reign supreme. Tailoring your strategy to prioritize mobile users ensures that your content is accessible, engaging, and primed for consumption, anytime and anywhere. This mobility not only elevates user engagement but also amplifies your potential for virality, setting the stage for profound growth and unprecedented reach in your social media endeavors.

Optimizing Content for Mobile Users

As we dive into the heart of developing a mobile-first strategy, it's pivotal to focus on optimizing content for mobile users. The shift towards mobile usage has been nothing short of revolutionary, turning smartphones into the primary gateway through which your audience interacts with your content. In this pursuit, understanding the nuances of mobile content consumption can set the stage for viral success on social media.

First and foremost, recognizing that mobile screens are smaller is a game-changer. This doesn't just mean that content needs to be legible; it needs to be captivating enough to grab and hold attention in a space where distractions abound. It's all about creating visually appealing content that can stop a thumb mid-swipe. High-quality, vivid images and crisp, concise videos become indispensable tools in your arsenal.

Let's talk about the speed of delivery. Mobile users are on the go, often seeking quick information or entertainment. Therefore, your content not only has to be compelling but also fast-loading. Heavy, slow-loading pages are your worst enemy, as they can lead to high bounce rates. Simple tweaks, like optimizing image sizes and minimizing the use of unnecessary scripts, can significantly enhance loading times.

Another key area is the adaptability of your content across different platforms. Given the variety of mobile devices and screen sizes, responsive design isn't optional; it's essential. Your content needs to look good and function well, whether it's viewed on a compact smartphone or a larger tablet. This adaptability extends to social media platforms themselves, tailoring your content to the unique specifications and best practices of each.

Interactive elements can also play a significant role in engaging mobile users. Polls, quizzes, and swipeable carousels leverage the tactile nature of mobile devices, encouraging active rather than passive consumption. These interactive features not only boost engagement but also increase the likelihood of your content being shared, amplifying its reach and potential for virality.

But don't overlook the power of concise, compelling copy. Mobile users often skim content, which means your message needs to be delivered quickly and clearly. Headlines should be attention-grabbing, and body text must be easy to digest in bite-sized pieces. This isn't the place for long paragraphs; instead, think snappy, impactful statements that drive your message home.

Accessibility is another critical consideration in optimizing content for mobile users. Ensure that your content is inclusive, considering factors like color contrast for readability and alt text for images. Making your content accessible not only broadens your audience but also enhances user experience, contributing to higher engagement and shareability.

Localization of content can't be ignored when targeting mobile users. Tailoring your content to local languages, cultures, and trends can dramatically improve its resonance with specific audiences. This approach can be particularly effective for platforms seeking to maximize their international reach and engagement.

The integration of social share buttons is a no-brainer yet often overlooked aspect of mobile content optimization. Making it effortless for users to share your content with a single tap can significantly increase its visibility and virality. Ensure these buttons are prominently placed but not intrusive, encouraging sharing without disrupting the user experience.

Understanding mobile user behavior is key to content optimization. Mobile analytics offer insights into how users interact with your content, enabling you to make data-driven decisions to enhance its performance. This involves analyzing metrics like engagement rates, time spent on content, and click-through rates, adjusting your strategy based on these insights.

Personalization of content is increasingly becoming a necessity. Mobile users expect content that resonates with their interests and needs. Leveraging data to offer personalized content recommendations can significantly enhance engagement and loyalty, making your social media platforms more relevant and attractive to your audience.

In the realm of social media, timing is everything, especially for mobile users. Posting your content when your audience is most active on their mobile devices increases visibility and engagement. Use analytics to determine these peak times and plan your content schedule accordingly.

Finally, the journey doesn't end with content creation. Encouraging and facilitating interaction through comments, shares, and direct messages turns content consumption into a conversation. Engaging with your audience in these interactions not only fosters community but also provides valuable feedback to further refine your mobile content strategy.

To wrap it up, optimizing content for mobile users is a multifaceted endeavor that requires attention to visual appeal, speed, responsiveness, and interaction. It's about creating a seamless, engaging, and personalized experience that resonates with your audience wherever they are. By putting mobile users at the forefront of your content strategy, you set the stage for broader reach, higher engagement, and, ultimately, viral success on social media.

Remember, in this mobile-first world, your ability to adapt and innovate in how you design and deliver your content can turn the small screen into your biggest opportunity. Embrace these principles, and watch your social media presence flourish in the palms of your audience's hands.

The Importance of Speed and Simplicity

In today's fast-paced world, where attention spans are shorter than ever, understanding the crucial role of speed and simplicity in your mobile-first strategy can make a significant difference. As we dive deep into developing strategies tailored for mobile users, it becomes evident that these two factors are not just important but essential for anyone looking to make an impact and go viral on social media. The reasons are straightforward - users demand quick, straightforward experiences that provide value without wasting time.

The essence of speed revolves around how swiftly your content loads and how quickly users can absorb the value from what you've posted. It's a known fact that mobile users tend to abandon websites or profiles that take too long to load. Every second counts, and the faster your content presents itself, the better your chances of keeping the audience engaged. This is crucial for growth and virality, as it aligns perfectly with the instant gratification needs of today's users.

Simplicity, on the other hand, refers to the ease with which users can navigate your content and understand your messages. A cluttered, complex presentation is likely to turn users away. The goal is to design content that speaks directly to the heart of the audience's needs and desires, eliminating any potential confusion. Simplicity in design and message can significantly amplify the impact of your content, making it more shareable and more likely to go viral.

When considering a mobile-first approach, it's imperative to optimize every aspect of your content for mobile users. This means considering the sizes of images and videos, the readability of text, and ensuring that interactive elements are easily accessible on touch screens. A mobile-optimized content strategy not only caters to the vast majority of social media users but also favors the algorithm, potentially boosting your visibility and reach.

Engagement metrics such as likes, shares, and comments are significantly influenced by how quickly and simply content is delivered. Users are more likely to interact with content that grabs their attention immediately and doesn't demand too much cognitive effort to digest. This interaction, in turn, plays a vital role in mastering the algorithm, as platforms tend to favor content with high engagement rates, pushing it to wider audiences.

The aspect of speed also translates into how rapidly you adapt to trends and user feedback. Virality often comes from jumping onto emerging trends at the right moment, which requires quick thinking and execution. Simplicity in your strategy here means having a clear, adaptable plan that allows you to leverage trends without compromising your core message or brand identity.

Moreover, simplicity in your content creation process allows for a more agile response to what's happening in your community and the world. It means employing tools and strategies that streamline content creation, enabling you to maintain a consistent presence without getting bogged down in complex processes. This consistency is key to building trust, engagement, and a sense of reliability among your followers.

In the landscape of social media, where algorithms change frequently and audience behaviors shift, a simple yet effective strategy can be your anchor. It ensures that regardless of external changes, your content remains accessible, engaging, and primely positioned for virality. Speed, in this context, means the ability to pivot and adapt quickly, ensuring your content strategy remains relevant and impactful.

From a monetization perspective, speed and simplicity can significantly boost your efforts. Fast, simple paths to purchase or learn more about a product or service can drastically increase conversion rates. Users are more likely to take action if the process is straightforward and quick. This is particularly important when leveraging social media for direct sales or lead generation, as complicated steps can lead to drop-offs and lost opportunities.

Understanding your audience's mobile usage patterns and preferences can further refine your strategy for speed and simplicity. This insight allows you to tailor your content delivery for maximum impact, whether it's optimizing posting times for when your audience is most active or simplifying messaging for clear, quick comprehension.

Additionally, the importance of speed and simplicity extends to your analytics and feedback mechanisms. Being able to quickly assess the performance of your content and simplify the data into actionable insights is crucial. This rapid analysis and implementation loop not only improves your strategy but also keeps you ahead in a competitive landscape.

Implementing a mobile-first strategy that emphasizes speed and simplicity can also have a significant impact on your brand's image. It portrays your brand as modern, efficient, and user-friendly, attributes highly valued by the digital audience. This perception can enhance your brand's appeal, attracting more followers and potential customers.

Lastly, the journey to mastering social media algorithms and achieving virality through a mobile-first strategy is an ongoing process. Emphasizing speed and simplicity does not mean compromising on quality. Instead, it's about smart optimization and focusing on what truly matters to your audience. This strategic focus is what can ultimately set you apart and help you build a lasting, impactful presence on social media.

In conclusion, speed and simplicity are not just cogs in the machine of mobile-first strategy; they're the very fuel that drives it. In the quest to grow, monetize, and go viral on social media, understanding and implementing these principles can be your roadmap to success. As you continue to navigate the ever-changing landscape of social media, keep these factors at the forefront of your strategy, and you'll find your path to virality becomes not just clearer, but achievable.

Engaging Audiences on the Go

In today's fast-paced digital landscape, developing a mobile-first strategy is no longer optional; it's imperative. As we delve deeper into optimizing our online presence for mobile users, we must focus on engaging audiences who are constantly on the move. The key lies in understanding how, when, and where people access content through their mobile devices and tailoring our strategies to meet these conditions.

First off, let's acknowledge the elephant in the room: attention spans are shrinking. This means that to grab and hold the attention of passersby in the digital realm, every piece of content we produce must be concise, compelling, and easily digestible. Think of your content as a digital snack—tasty, satisfying, but not overwhelming.

Moreover, the design of your content plays a critical role in mobile engagement. Users scrolling on their phones are less likely to stop for a chunk of text than they are for a visually appealing image or a quick, engaging video. Leveraging multimedia content isn't just a recommendation; it's a necessity for engaging audiences on the go.

Another crucial aspect to consider is the loading time of your content. Mobile users are often in environments with varying levels of internet speed. Ensuring your content loads quickly on all types of connections is crucial to prevent potential viewers from scrolling past in frustration. Remember, speed and simplicity are your best friends in the mobile-first world.

Interactivity also plays a significant role in engaging mobile audiences. Features such as polls, swipe-up links, and interactive stories not only make consuming content more engaging but also create opportunities for audiences to actively participate. Such engagement cements your content in the viewer's memory, making them more likely to recall and interact with your brand in the future.

Let's not forget the importance of optimizing for different platforms. The mobile experience varies widely across social media apps. Tailoring content to fit the format and community of each platform can dramatically increase engagement and visibility. This means understanding the nuances of what works on Instagram versus TikTok or Facebook and adjusting accordingly.

Timing is another element that cannot be overlooked. Knowing when your audience is most likely to be on their phone and active on social media can significantly increase the chances of your content being seen. Utilize analytics tools to track when your posts receive the most engagement and plan your content schedule around these peak times.

Localization of content is also key to engaging a mobile audience. Mobile users are often looking for information or entertainment that resonates with their local context. Tailoring your message to fit local languages, trends, and cultural nuances can make your content more relevant and engaging to viewers in specific regions.

User-generated content (UGC) is a powerful tool for engaging audiences on mobile devices. Encouraging your followers to share their own stories, images, or videos related to your brand not only provides you with authentic content to repost but also fosters a community feeling. UGC can increase trust in your brand and encourage more interaction from your audience.

Push notifications can be a double-edged sword. Used wisely, they can draw users back to your app or profile by alerting them to new content or exclusive offers. However, overuse can lead to annoyance and app deletion. Make sure your notifications offer real value and are sent at appropriate times.

Accessibility should also be top of mind when engaging audiences on the go. Ensure that your content is accessible to people with disabilities by adding captions to videos, using voiceovers, and ensuring your website and social media profiles comply with accessibility guidelines. This not only broadens your audience but also demonstrates your brand's commitment to inclusivity.

Consistency is crucial in building a loyal mobile audience. Your content should consistently reflect your brand's tone, style, and values across all platforms. Regular posting schedules, consistent interaction with followers, and a stable content theme help build a recognizable and reliable presence that audiences can look forward to engaging with.

Lastly, the power of simplicity cannot be understated. In your quest to engage mobile audiences, it's easy to get carried away with complex features or detailed content. However, the most successful mobile content often embodies simplicity—clear, straightforward messages paired with strong visuals that convey the desired action or emotion at a glance.

Embracing a mobile-first strategy and engaging audiences on the go requires a blend of creativity, agility, and strategic thinking. The mobile landscape is ever-evolving, and so should our approaches to engaging with audiences within it. By focusing on delivering value, enhancing user experience, and fostering community, we can captivate and grow our mobile audience in meaningful ways.

As we wrap up this section, remember that the journey to engaging mobile audiences is ongoing. Continuous learning, testing, and adapting are part of the process. Keep your finger on the pulse of emerging mobile trends and technologies, and always be ready to refine your strategy to meet your audience where they are—on their phones, navigating through their fast-paced digital lives.

Chapter 19:
Building a Global Community

In the age of digital ubiquity, transforming your social media platforms into a vibrant, global community is not just an ambition—it's a strategic necessity. Harnessing the power of social media groups becomes your first order of business. It's about carving out spaces where your audience not only sees your content but feels a part of the conversation, sharing their thoughts, photos, and experiences. This is where the magic of user-generated content comes in. Encourage your followers to tag your brand, use your campaign hashtags, and share how your product or brand plays a role in their lives. This not only enriches your content pool but builds authenticity and trust among your audience.

But how do you take this community and give it a global footprint? The answer lies in strategies for global engagement. It's about recognizing and celebrating the diversity within your community. Tailoring your content to include different cultural perspectives or acknowledging global events and holidays can make your brand more relatable and inclusive. It's also about being active and responsive; engage with comments, questions, and content shared by your community members from different parts of the world—even if it means hopping onto Google Translate to do so. Through these strategies, your social media platform can transform from a broadcasting channel into a dynamic, global community, bound not by geography, but by shared interests and mutual respect.

Harnessing the Power of Social Media Groups

In the expansive world of social media, groups have emerged as pivotal arenas for fostering vibrant communities and driving meaningful engagement. As one navigates the quest to build a global community, understanding and leveraging the potential of social media groups is non-negotiable. This chapter delves into the strategies and insights essential for harnessing the power of these platforms, turning online gatherings into thriving ecosystems for brand expansion.

At the heart of social media groups lies the opportunity for targeted interaction. These digital alcoves provide a unique chance to engage directly with a specific segment of your audience, one that shares common interests or needs. By focusing on these micro-communities, you're able to tailor your content, dialogue, and marketing efforts in a way that resonates deeply, fostering a sense of belonging and loyalty among members.

Creating or joining the right group requires strategic thought. It's essential to align your social media endeavors with groups that reflect your brand's ethos and appeal to your target demographic. Participation in or management of a group should be driven by objectives: whether it's to increase awareness, drive sales, or establish authority within a niche. Setting clear goals at the outset will guide your actions and help measure success.

Moderation is the cornerstone of a thriving social media group. A well-managed group promotes healthy interaction, ensuring conversations remain constructive and aligned with the group's purpose. The role of a moderator extends beyond policing content; it's about sparking discussions, encouraging member participation, and keeping the community engaged. This active oversight helps cultivate an environment where members feel valued and invested.

Content is king, even within the microcosm of social media groups. Tailoring content to the specific interests of your group's demographic can significantly boost engagement rates. This could mean offering exclusive insights, sharing behind-the-scenes content, or providing early access to new products or services. Remember, the content that feels personal and exclusive fosters a stronger connection and loyalty among group members.

Engagement should never be a one-way street. Encouraging members to share their own stories, experiences, or content can transform your group from a passive audience to an active community. This user-generated content not only enriches the group's dialogue but also provides valuable insights into your audience's preferences, challenges, and expectations.

The power of social media groups extends beyond engagement; they are potent tools for feedback and customer insight. Opening lines of communication for product feedback, testimonials, or general suggestions can provide direct access to what your audience truly wants. This immediate and often candid feedback is gold dust for refining your offerings and tailoring your strategies to match your audience's needs.

Collaborations within and across groups can exponentially increase your reach. Partnering with influencers, thought leaders, or other brands within your niche can introduce your brand to new audiences. These collaborations should offer mutual benefit, providing value to all participating parties and their respective audiences.

Exclusive events or promotions for group members can significantly enhance the value of belonging to your community. Whether it's a live Q&A session, a webinar, or access to exclusive deals, these special offerings elevate the group experience, making membership feel like a VIP pass.

Measuring the success of your group engagement is crucial. Just like any other marketing effort, the activities within social media groups should be analyzed for performance. Engagement rates, growth in membership, and the quality of interactions provide insights into the health and impact of your community-building efforts. Tools and analytics provided by social media platforms can aid in this assessment, offering a quantifiable look at your strategies' effectiveness.

Feedback loops between your broader social media strategy and your group activities are vital. Insights gleaned from group interactions should inform your overall social media content strategy, ensuring it remains responsive to your audience's evolving needs. This dynamic approach allows for a cohesive and integrated marketing effort that speaks directly to the heart of your audience.

Privacy and respect are paramount within social media groups. It's essential to create a safe space where members feel comfortable sharing without fear of judgment or privacy breaches. Clear guidelines and strict adherence to privacy policies not only protect members but also build trust in your brand.

Adaptability is key in the ever-evolving landscape of social media. Groups that remain responsive to changes in platform algorithms, member preferences, and global trends are more likely to thrive. Staying informed and flexible allows you to pivot your strategies as needed, ensuring your community remains engaged and your brand stays relevant.

Ultimately, the success of leveraging social media groups in building a global community hinges on genuine interest and consistent effort. It's not merely about numbers but about cultivating a space where meaningful interactions can flourish, driving engagement, loyalty, and growth. By prioritizing the needs and interests of your group members, you create a foundation for a robust and thriving community.

In conclusion, harnessing the power of social media groups is an art form that requires insight, dedication, and a deep understanding of your audience. As you embark on this journey, keep in mind the essential role these groups play in connecting your brand with its most passionate followers. With the right approach, social media groups can be transformed into vibrant communities that significantly contribute to your brand's global impact and success.

Encouraging User-Generated Content

In the modern tapestry of social media, encouraging user-generated content (UGC) isn't just a strategy; it's a powerful cornerstone for building a global community. It's about flipping the script, turning your audience from passive viewers into active participants. Here's how to transform your followers into creators alongside you, and why it's a game-changer for your social media journey.

Firstly, understand what user-generated content truly is. It's any form of content—be it text, videos, images, reviews, etc.—created by users rather than brands. Now, why does this matter? When followers contribute content, they're engaging with your brand on a deeper level. This not only boosts your content supply but enhances its authenticity—a currency of immense value in the social media realm.

One of the most potent ways to kickstart UGC is through contests and challenges. Design a challenge that's fun, easily shareable, and relevant to your niche. Use a specific hashtag to track submissions and offer a compelling incentive for participation. This strategy does not only foster community engagement but often leads to viral moments, amplifying your reach exponentially.

Hashtags are your best friend in the UGC journey. They're not just a tool to organize content; they're a rallying cry for your community to unite under. Create a branded hashtag that encapsulates your community's ethos. It should be memorable, unique, and inviting. This hashtag becomes a repository of your community's creativity and a visual testament to your collective identity.

Feedback is a two-way street. When users take the time to create content related to your brand, recognize their effort. Feature their content on your platforms, comment on their posts, or shout them out in your stories. This recognition not only rewards their effort but serves as an incentive for others to join in.

Transparency is key. When asking for UGC, be clear about how you intend to use it. Your community values honesty, and transparent communication fosters trust—a crucial element in encouraging participation. Whether it's for a contest, a testimonial, or a featured post, ensure your guidelines are straightforward and your intentions are clear.

Another avenue to explore is collaborations with influencers or creators in your niche. They can inspire their followers to create content for your brand, offering a fresh angle and tapping into their audience. However, choose collaborators who align with your brand values to maintain integrity and authenticity in your UGC efforts.

Empower with tools and resources. Sometimes, your community is eager to create but unsure how. Offering tips, ideas, or even tools can empower them to contribute. This could be as simple as sharing content creation tips, providing templates, or hosting a webinar on creating engaging social media content.

Embed UGC in your content strategy. User-generated content shouldn't be an afterthought. Plan your content calendar with spaces for UGC to shine. Whether it's a weekly feature or part of a larger campaign, integrating UGC seamlessly into your content strategy elevates its importance and encourages more participation.

Quality matters. Encourage high-quality submissions by setting clear guidelines and offering examples of outstanding UGC. This elevates the overall perception of your brand and inspires others to put more effort into their contributions. Quality UGC can serve as powerful testimonials and endorsements, further amplifying your brand's credibility.

Leverage storytelling. Prompt your community to share their stories related to your brand or products. This humanizes your brand, making it more relatable and strengthening the emotional connection with your audience. Personal stories have a unique way of resonating with others, fostering a sense of belonging and community.

Remember, patience is a virtue. Building a UGC-rich community doesn't happen overnight. It's a process that requires nurturing, engagement, and consistent effort. Celebrate the milestones, appreciate the contributors, and remain committed to fostering an environment that encourages creativity and participation.

Feedback loops are essential. Engage with the community not just by acknowledging their contributions but by seeking their input on what they'd like to see more of. This not only gives you insights into their preferences but makes them feel valued and integral to your brand's journey.

Finally, make it inclusive. Your call for user-generated content should invite participation from all segments of your audience. Create opportunities for diverse contributions, ensuring that your community feels seen, heard, and valued. Inclusivity not only enriches your content pool but strengthens your community's bond.

In conclusion, encouraging user-generated content is about much more than just generating free content for your social media platforms. It's about building deeper relationships with your community, amplifying authenticity, and fostering a vibrant, engaged global audience. By applying these strategies, you're not just growing your social media presence; you're cultivating a passionate community eager to join you on this journey.

Strategies for Global Engagement

In the grand tapestry of social media, weaving a narrative that resonates on a global scale is both an art and a science. As we explore strategies for global engagement, remember that the core of social media is connection—across cities, countries, and continents. Engaging globally doesn't just mean reaching more people; it means connecting with them in ways that are meaningful, respectful, and mutually beneficial.

First and foremost, understanding cultural nuances is paramount. What captivates an audience in one region may not translate well in another. This requires a balance of universal content that appeals to broad human emotions and targeted content that acknowledges and respects cultural differences. It's about striking a chord that resonates universally, yet tailoring the nuance to fit the locale.

Localization goes beyond mere translation. Yes, translating your content into other languages can significantly increase your reach, but localization digs deeper. It involves adapting your content to reflect local customs, values, and humour. This might mean creating entirely different content for different regions, but the payoff in engagement and loyalty is worth the effort.

Time zones play a curious role in global engagement. Posting when your audience is asleep won't do you any favours. Use analytics to understand where your audience is and schedule your content accordingly. This might mean employing a staggered posting schedule that ensures you hit the peak engagement windows across different time zones.

Utilizing global trends can catapult your content into the international limelight. However, tread carefully. It's essential to understand the context behind a trend to ensure your engagement is appropriate and respectful. Harnessing a global trend involves adding value to the conversation, not just hopping on the bandwagon for the sake of visibility.

Collaboration is a powerful tool for global engagement. Partner with influencers or brands from different regions to tap into their audience. This not only broadens your reach but also lends credibility to your brand in new markets. Choose collaborators who align with your values and goals for the most authentic and effective partnerships.

User-generated content (UGC) is a goldmine for global engagement. Encourage your audience to share their own stories, photos, or videos related to your brand. Not only does this provide authentic content that speaks directly to different audiences, but it also fosters a sense of community and belonging among your followers.

Hashtags can serve as a bridge to global audiences. Use a mix of popular global hashtags and specific local tags to increase your content's discoverability. Researching and using the right hashtags can place your content in front of a global audience ready to engage with topics they're passionate about.

Localization of social media platforms is another aspect that cannot be overlooked. Certain platforms dominate specific regions. Understanding which platforms are preferred in different parts of the world and establishing a presence there can significantly boost your global reach.

Data-driven strategies are crucial in understanding what works and what doesn't on a global scale. Leverage analytics to track engagement across different regions and refine your strategy accordingly.

Experimentation is key—try different approaches and content types to see what resonates most with international audiences.

The tone and messaging of your content play a significant role in global engagement. A respectful, inclusive tone that acknowledges diversity and promotes unity is more likely to be embraced on a global scale. Remember, social media is a platform for building bridges, not walls.

Visuals transcend language barriers. Investing in high-quality, visually appealing content can captivate a global audience even before they read the caption. Whether it's stunning photography, engaging videos, or eye-catching graphics, visuals are a universal language that can draw people in from across the globe.

Responsiveness to global events and sensitivity to their implications is crucial. While engaging with current events can increase relevance and relatability, it's important to approach such topics with empathy and understanding. Being seen as opportunistic or insensitive can damage your brand on an international level.

Lastly, fostering a global community requires patience and persistence. Building genuine connections and understanding with a diverse audience doesn't happen overnight. It requires consistent effort, a willingness to learn and adapt, and an unwavering commitment to respect and inclusivity.

In conclusion, global engagement on social media is not just about expanding your reach; it's about connecting with and understanding the diverse tapestry of humanity that makes up your audience. By employing strategies that respect cultural nuances, adapt to local preferences, and promote genuine connections, you can create a truly global community that supports and amplifies your brand on the international stage.

Chapter 20:
Navigating Algorithm Updates

In the whirlwind world of social media, staying static means falling behind, especially when it comes to algorithm updates. Algorithms aren't just background technology; they're the gatekeepers of your content's visibility and engagement. The key to mastering these ever-evolving beasts lies in flexibility and a robust understanding of platform analytics. It's about knowing when to tweak your content strategy, when to double down on what's working, and when to pivot entirely. Keeping your thumb on the pulse of these updates can feel like a full-time job, but it's essential. Instead of seeing algorithm changes as hurdles, view them as opportunities to innovate and stand out. Diversify your content to cater to different aspects of the algorithm, such as incorporating more video content if the platform is favoring that medium. Engage with your audience to understand what resonates with them, using their feedback as a compass for content creation. Remember, learning from each algorithm change can provide invaluable insights into your audience's preferences and content consumption habits, which is gold for anyone aiming to go viral and grow their social media presence. Adaptability, strategic content planning, and an analytical mindset are your best allies in navigating the turbulent waters of social media algorithms.

Staying Ahead of the Curve

In the world of social media, the only constant is change. Platforms regularly update their algorithms in a relentless pursuit of improving user experience and increasing engagement. For content creators aiming to go viral and monetize their social media presence, staying ahead of these changes is not just beneficial—it's crucial. This section explores strategies to keep you at the forefront of algorithm updates, ensuring your content continues to reach and resonate with your audience.

First and foremost, understanding the basics of how algorithms work is a foundational step. Social media platforms are essentially trying to show users the content they believe is most relevant and engaging. Although the specific mechanics can seem like a closely guarded secret, the general principles of relevance, engagement, and user satisfaction are key. Keeping these principles in mind when creating content can help align your strategy with the goals of the algorithms.

Engagement is the currency of social media. Algorithms favor content that sparks interactions—likes, comments, shares, and views. Therefore, encouraging your audience to engage with your posts isn't just about building a community; it's about increasing your content's visibility. Ask questions, solicit feedback, and create content that prompts response. Engagement breeds further engagement, creating a virtuous cycle that algorithms recognize and reward.

Being adaptable is equally important. When an algorithm update occurs, it can significantly affect your content's performance. Creators who quickly adapt their strategies can mitigate negative impacts or even capitalize on changes. This requires staying informed about updates and being willing to experiment with your content and engagement strategies. Sometimes, even a small tweak in how you post or interact can yield significantly better results under a new algorithm.

Analytics are your ally in understanding the effects of algorithm changes. Platforms provide a wealth of data that can help you decipher what works and what doesn't. Regularly review your analytics to identify trends, anomalies, or shifts in engagement and reach. This data can provide early indicators of how algorithm changes are affecting your content, allowing you to adjust accordingly.

Diversifying your content types can also protect your social media presence against the whims of algorithm changes. If you're heavily reliant on one type of content, an algorithm update that de-emphasizes that content could be devastating. Incorporating a variety of content types—photos, videos, live streams, stories—can help safeguard your reach and engagement against these shifts.

Building genuine connections with your audience goes beyond superficial engagement metrics. When you foster a community around your content, you create a dedicated group of followers who will seek out your posts, regardless of algorithm changes. This isn't to say that algorithms won't affect your visibility, but a committed audience can be a stabilizing force in the face of change.

Staying informed about potential and actual updates is a proactive way to stay ahead. Follow industry news, participate in creator forums, and pay attention to official announcements from social media platforms. Knowledge is power, and in the context of navigating algorithm updates, it's your first line of defense.

Experimentation is not just beneficial; it's essential. The algorithms are constantly learning and evolving, which means what worked yesterday might not work tomorrow. Regularly testing different types of content, posting times, and engagement strategies can help you understand what resonates best with your audience and the algorithm.

It's also important to focus on creating timeless content. While trends can give you a temporary boost in visibility, focusing too much on them can make your content quickly feel outdated. Timeless, evergreen content can continue to perform well over time, providing value regardless of algorithm shifts.

Learning from others can provide valuable insights into adapting to algorithm changes. Analyze competitors and industry leaders to see how they adjust their strategies in response to updates. While not every strategy will be applicable to your situation, observing the field can spark ideas and provide strategic direction.

Participating in beta features and new platform offerings can give you an edge. Platforms often favor early adopters of new features in the algorithm, as they're keen to promote these innovations. Keeping an eye out for these opportunities and being among the first to utilize them can give your content a temporary boost.

Lastly, remember that your value doesn't solely come from mastering the algorithm. The core of your social media success lies in the quality and relevance of the content you create and the relationships you build with your audience. While algorithms play a significant role in how content is discovered and seen, they are ultimately tools to help deliver your content to those who find it most relevant and engaging.

Staying ahead of algorithm updates requires a blend of strategic planning, adaptability, and a deep understanding of your audience. By focusing on these key areas, you can navigate the ever-changing landscape of social media, ensuring that your content continues to thrive, regardless of the technical tweaks made behind the scenes.

In conclusion, navigating the world of social media algorithms is a journey, not a destination. As platforms evolve, so too should your strategies. By staying informed, adaptable, and focused on creating meaningful engagement, you can not only stay ahead of the curve but also capitalize on the opportunities that algorithm changes present. Ultimately, the goal is to use these changes to your advantage, crafting content that resonates, engages, and achieves your objectives in the dynamic world of social media.

Adapting Content and Strategies

As we dive into the realm of adapting content and strategies, it's crucial to remember that staying flexible and alert is the backbone of mastering social media algorithms. As these algorithms evolve, so must our approach to content creation and distribution. Let's explore how to stay ahead of the curve and keep your content fresh and engaging.

First off, it's fundamental to keep a close eye on your analytics. These numbers are your road map to understanding what's working and what isn't. If you notice a dip in engagement or reach, that's your cue to pivot. This might mean tweaking your content mix, experimenting with new formats, or adjusting your posting schedule. Remember, data doesn't lie, and it's your best tool in navigating the ever-changing social media landscape.

An essential element in adapting your strategies is to continuously experiment. The digital world thrives on innovation, and sometimes, a simple change in your approach can yield significant results. Whether it's incorporating new hashtags, engaging with trending topics, or trying out emerging platforms, staying adaptable means you're always ready to ride the wave of the next big thing.

Engaging with your community is another key strategy. As algorithms prioritize content that sparks conversations and interactions, fostering a strong connection with your followers becomes even more vital. Ask questions, encourage feedback, and truly listen to what they have to say. This two-way communication not only boosts your engagement rates but also provides invaluable insights into your audience's preferences and interests.

Investing time in understanding the intricacies of each social media platform can also pay off. Each platform has its unique algorithm, and a strategy that works wonders on Instagram might not necessarily translate to success on YouTube. Tailor your content and tactics to fit the platform you're targeting, keeping in mind the specific preferences of its user base.

Another tactic to adapt your strategy is leveraging user-generated content (UGC). UGC not only provides you with fresh, authentic content but also significantly boosts engagement and trust among your audience. Encourage your followers to share their experiences with your brand or create content around themes related to your niche. This not only diversifies your content but also strengthens your community.

Staying updated with the latest features and tools offered by social media platforms can give you an edge. Platforms frequently roll out new features to keep users engaged and entertained. By being among the first to use these features, you can set your content apart and capture the attention of both your existing audience and potential new followers.

Diversifying your content strategy is equally important. Don't put all your eggs in one basket. If you solely rely on one type of content or a single platform, you're putting your online presence at risk. Explore different content formats - from blogs and videos to podcasts and infographics. Spreading your content across multiple channels increases your visibility and reduces the impact of algorithm changes on any single platform.

Collaboration with other creators and brands can also breathe new life into your content strategy. These partnerships can introduce your work to new audiences, providing a fresh perspective and injecting creativity into your content. Additionally, collaborations are often favored by algorithms because they generate high levels of engagement.

Lastly, never underestimate the power of a compelling narrative. Storytelling has been a captivating tool long before the age of social media and continues to be an effective way to engage audiences. Share behind-the-scenes glimpses, success and failure stories, or customer testimonials. Authentic stories resonate with followers and can significantly enhance your content's appeal.

Being mindful of the tone and voice of your content is crucial. Your audience likely follows you because they resonate with your personality or brand voice. Even as you adapt your content and strategies, ensure your core messaging and tone remain consistent. Consistency breeds familiarity and trust, which are invaluable in building a loyal following.

Considering the global reach of social media, think about inclusivity in your content. This might mean creating content that speaks to different cultural contexts or is accessible to people with disabilities. An inclusive approach not only broadens your potential audience but also reflects positively on your brand's values.

Embracing the power of storytelling in various formats can also drive engagement. For instance, Stories, Reels, or TikToks offer dynamic ways to share content that is both engaging and ephemeral. These formats often favor spontaneity and authenticity, adding a personal touch to your online presence.

Educating yourself continuously is non-negotiable in the up-and-down world of social media. Attend webinars, read industry blogs, or join online communities of content creators. The collective wisdom and experiences shared in these spaces can provide unique insights and strategies for tackling algorithm changes.

In wrapping up, remember that while algorithms may dictate the playfield, it's creativity, adaptability, and genuine engagement that win the game. By staying informed, being willing to pivot your strategies, and keeping your audience at the heart of your content, you can navigate the challenges of social media's ever-evolving algorithms with confidence and success.

Learning From Algorithm Changes

Experiencing shifts and adjustments in social media algorithms can feel like navigating through a maze without a clear guide. However, these alterations aren't roadblocks but rather signposts for innovation and growth in your social media strategy. Every algorithm update brings with it a lesson, and understanding these lessons is crucial for anyone looking to go viral, grow their following, and ultimately monetize their social media presence.

Firstly, it's essential to recognize that algorithm changes are made with the user experience in mind. Social media platforms aim to present content that is relevant, engaging, and likely to satisfy users' interests and needs. When an algorithm changes, it signals a shift in what the platform values in content. By analyzing these shifts, you can glean insights into the type of content you should produce to align with these new preferences.

Engagement metrics often undergo recalibration during algorithm updates. For instance, a platform may emphasize the importance of comments over likes, signaling the value of creating content that encourages discussions. This realization should prompt you to craft posts that are not just visually appealing but also compelling enough to initiate conversations among your followers.

Another important aspect to consider is the diversification of content types. With each algorithm update, platforms may prioritize different content formats, such as live videos, stories, or carousel posts. Experimenting with these formats can not only help your content gain visibility under the new algorithm but also provide insights into what resonates most with your audience.

The frequency and timing of your posts can also be impacted by algorithm changes. Sometimes, what worked in the past in terms of when and how often you post may no longer yield the same results.

Paying close attention to your engagement metrics post-update can help you identify new optimal posting schedules that cater to your audience's current online habits.

Moreover, algorithm updates can lead to changes in content discovery mechanisms, such as hashtag usage or the exploration of new topics. Keeping a pulse on these modifications can guide you in tweaking your content strategy to ensure your posts are discoverable by a wider audience.

Personalization has become a cornerstone of social media algorithms, emphasizing the need to create content that speaks directly to your audience's preferences. Updates may enhance the platform's ability to match content with users' interests, making it even more vital to understand your audience deeply and tailor your content accordingly.

It's also crucial to engage in continuous learning and keep abreast of industry news. Platforms often provide resources and updates about new algorithm changes. Engaging with these resources, alongside following industry experts and participating in professional communities, can provide valuable insights and tips for adapting your strategy.

Algorithm changes oftentimes reevaluate the importance of authenticity and originality in content creation. This underscores the necessity of investing time and thought into producing unique content that not only adheres to the algorithm's criteria but also sets you apart from competitors.

Utilizing analytics tools to decipher how your content is performing before and after an algorithm update can offer concrete data on what to adapt or maintain in your strategy. These tools can highlight trends and patterns that may not be immediately obvious, guiding your content tweaks and strategy refinements.

Remember, while algorithms dictate content distribution, it's the users who dictate success. Creating content that is genuine, valuable, and engaging should always be at the heart of your strategy, no matter how algorithms evolve. Focusing on your audience's needs and preferences will always favor you in the dynamic landscape of social media.

Adapting to algorithm changes also means embracing flexibility in your approach. Being too rigid in content creation and distribution methods may hinder your ability to pivot quickly and effectively. Cultivating a mindset of adaptability and resilience can make navigating these updates less daunting and more opportunistic.

Collaboration with other creators can also unveil diverse perspectives on navigating algorithm changes. Sharing experiences and strategies with peers can expose you to novel ideas and tactics that you might not have considered, enriching your approach to content creation and distribution.

Finally, it's essential to maintain a long-term perspective when adapting to algorithm changes. Immediate results may not always be visible, but consistency, persistence, and a willingness to evolve your strategy over time can lead to sustainable growth and success on social media platforms.

In conclusion, while algorithm updates may seem like challenges at first, they offer valuable opportunities for growth, learning, and innovation. By staying informed, being adaptable, and focusing on creating meaningful connections with your audience, you can navigate these changes successfully and continue to thrive in the ever-evolving world of social media.

Chapter 21:
Beyond Social Media:
Expanding Your Digital Presence

In an era where your digital footprint is as critical as your real-world presence, it's important to diversify your online platforms. While your social media channels are the frontline of engaging with your audience, integrating these with a well-designed blog or website can amplify your reach and deepen connections. Think of your website as your digital headquarters, where you control the narrative, unfiltered by algorithm changes. Plus, owning your content safeguards against the ephemeral nature of social media platforms. Transitioning into email marketing, remember it's not just about sending newsletters but about forging personal connections through tailored content that adds value, thereby nurturing a loyal community that translates into tangible success metrics.

Moreover, tapping into the synergy between social media and e-commerce opens up a direct revenue stream. Your social platforms can serve as a funnel, guiding followers to your website where they can make purchases, subscribe to services, or engage more deeply with your brand. This interconnected digital ecosystem – comprising social media, a compelling website, strategic email marketing, and a seamless e-commerce experience – not only maximizes your online visibility but also bolsters your brand's credibility and fosters sustainable growth. By mastering the art of integrating these elements, you're not just surviving; you're thriving in the digital age, creating a multifaceted presence that resonates with your audience across platforms.

Integrating Social Media With Blogs and Websites

When you're diving into the deep end of building your digital empire, one thing becomes crystal clear: your social media hustle needs to be about more than just social media. It's like throwing a wider net to catch more fish. You've already got the bait – your content; now, it's time to spread it across different platforms to maximize your catch. This is where integrating social media with blogs and websites comes into play, creating a cohesive online presence that can significantly amplify your reach and influence.

Think of your website or blog as home base. It's the heart of your digital empire, a place where you have total control over the narrative. Unlike social media platforms, which are at the mercy of ever-changing algorithms, your website is yours alone. Here, you can house everything from detailed blog posts to an online store, weaving in your social media content to create a rich, interactive experience for your audience.

Integrating social media isn't just about slapping social icons on your homepage or having a feed widget in the footer. It's about creating seamless pathways for your audience to move between your social channels and your website. For instance, using blog posts to dive deeper into topics you've touched on in social posts can draw your audience further into your ecosystem, encouraging them to spend more time with your content.

Another key aspect is content synchronization. What you share on social media should not exist in a vacuum. By highlighting social media posts in your blog content, or vice versa, you're not just cross-promoting; you're creating a multi-dimensional content experience.

This doesn't just boost your content's value; it can also significantly improve SEO, driving more organic traffic to your site.

Let's talk about the art of the call to action (CTA). Your social media can serve as a dynamic billboard for your blog or website, encouraging your followers to explore more deeply. Crafting compelling CTAs isn't just about telling your audience to click a link; it's about offering them value that they can only get by taking the next step. Whether it's a detailed guide, an exclusive video, or a special offer, your CTAs should be irresistible.

User-generated content (UGC) can be a goldmine for enhancing your website. Featuring reviews, comments, or contributions from your social media followers not only enriches your site's content but also builds a sense of community. It shows that you're listening and engaging with your audience, turning your site into a collaborative space.

Analytics should be your best friend in this integration process. Tracking how social media drives traffic to your website can offer valuable insights into what content resonates with your audience. Adjust your strategy based on hard data, and you'll find more effective ways to connect and engage with your followers across platforms.

Email sign-ups are another crucial piece of the puzzle. By integrating options for visitors to subscribe to your newsletter or email list via social media and your website, you're building a direct line of communication. This is prime real estate for deeper engagement, allowing you to nurture your audience with personalized content and offers.

Don't overlook the importance of consistency in branding across your social media and website. Consistency builds trust and recognition. Ensure that your visual branding, voice, and messaging are uniform across all platforms. This consistency makes your digital presence feel professional and cohesive, reinforcing your brand identity with every interaction.

Integrating social media with your website isn't a one-and-done deal; it's an ongoing process of optimization and adaptation. Digital trends are constantly evolving, and so should your strategy. Keep experimenting with new ways to weave your social media presence into your website, and remain flexible enough to pivot your approach as needed.

Collaborations can also tap into a new audience. Featuring guest posts on your blog from influencers in your niche or collaborating on social media content can introduce your brand to new eyes. This not just diversifies your content but also builds credibility through association.

The synergy between your social media and website should also extend to e-commerce if you're selling products or services. Integrating social reviews, sharing customer testimonials, and showcasing products on both platforms can significantly boost your sales. Think of social proof; it's a powerful tool for converting followers into customers.

Let's not forget about the potential for exclusive content. Offering something unique to your website visitors that isn't available on your social media channels can be a huge draw. This could be in-depth articles, e-books, or even webinars. The idea is to provide value that encourages your social media followers to cross over to your website.

Lastly, engaging with your audience through comments and interactions both on social media and your website solidifies your community. It shows you're not just broadcasting messages but are genuinely interested in a two-way conversation. This level of engagement can foster a loyal following that's more likely to support your monetization efforts.

In conclusion, integrating your social media with your blog or website is not just beneficial; it's essential for anyone looking to expand their digital presence. It's about creating a cohesive ecosystem where your content thrives, engagement deepens, and your digital empire grows. With strategic integration, your journey from social media star to digital mogul is not just possible; it's inevitable.

Email Marketing Strategies

As we broaden our digital presence beyond just social media, it's vital to tap into the proven power of email marketing. While social platforms allow us to catch the eye of the audience momentarily, emails open the door to a more intimate and direct form of communication. Think of it as the difference between catching someone's attention in a crowded room and having a one-on-one conversation with them. Both are valuable, but they serve different purposes.

First things first, building a substantial email list is your initial goal. But how? Leverage your existing social media presence. Use your posts, stories, and bio links to encourage your followers to sign up for your emails. Offer them something irresistible in return, like exclusive content, a first look at your new products, or a valuable downloadable resource. Remember, the incentive needs to align with your audience's interests.

Personalization is no longer just an option; it's a necessity in today's email marketing strategies. With tools at your disposal to segment your audience based on their behavior, preferences, and engagement history, sending out blanket emails should be a thing of the past. Imagine tailoring emails that resonate personally with each segment of your audience. The result? Higher open rates, improved click-through rates, and a deeper connection with your subscribers.

Let's talk content. What you send is just as important as how you send it. Yes, the ultimate goal might be to sell a product or promote a service, but if every email screams "buy this," you'll quickly see your unsubscribe rate climb. Balance is key. Your emails should educate, entertain, or inspire your readers just as much as they promote. Share stories, insights, behind-the-scenes looks, and valuable information that keeps your audience reading.

The subject line of your email is your first impression—it's what stands between your beautifully crafted email and the dreaded delete button. Think of it as the headline of a news article or the title of a blog post. It needs to grab attention, spark curiosity, or promise value. A/B testing different subject lines can help you understand what resonates best with your audience, guiding your strategy moving forward.

Email marketing isn't fire-and-forget. Analyzing the performance of your campaigns is crucial. Pay attention to open rates, click-through rates, and conversion rates. But also, dig deeper. Look at the times of day your emails perform best, the type of content that drives engagement, and even the links within your email that are clicked on the most. This data isn't just numbers—it's a roadmap to refining your strategy and achieving better results.

Automation tools can be a game-changer for your email marketing efforts. They allow you to schedule emails, send out birthday wishes, and even trigger specific emails based on subscriber actions, like abandoning a cart on your e-commerce site. But remember, automation doesn't mean your emails should lose their personal touch. Even automated emails should feel as though they're coming directly from you to your subscriber.

Design matters in email marketing. In a world where our inboxes are flooded daily, the visual appeal of your email can make it stand out. Use high-quality images, play with layouts, and ensure your brand's personality shines through. However, be mindful of loading times and readability across devices—your emails need to look good on everything from a desktop computer to a smartphone screen.

Don't forget about the call to action (CTA). Every email you send should have an objective, whether it's to drive traffic to your latest blog post, encourage sign-ups for an event, or promote a new product launch. Your CTA should be clear, compelling, and easy to find. Sometimes, tweaking the wording or the design of your CTA can significantly impact the effectiveness of your email.

Email marketing also offers a perfect opportunity to experiment with storytelling. Unlike social media, where content is often consumed in a fast-paced and fragmented way, emails allow you to take your reader on a journey. Use this space to tell stories about your brand, share customer testimonials, or highlight the impact your products or services have made. Storytelling not only engages but also builds loyalty and trust.

Privacy and compliance are not to be taken lightly. With laws like GDPR in Europe and similar regulations popping up globally, it's essential to ensure that your email marketing practices are up to standard. This means obtaining explicit consent to send emails, providing clear unsubscribe options, and managing your subscriber data securely. Respecting your subscribers' privacy is not only a legal obligation but also builds trust.

Integrating your email marketing with your social media strategy can amplify your results. Use your emails to encourage subscribers to follow you on social media platforms, and vice versa. This creates multiple touchpoints with your audience, increasing the opportunity for engagement, sales, and even customer retention. Keep in mind, cohesion across platforms strengthens your brand identity and message.

Don't overlook the importance of timing in your email marketing strategy. While it's crucial to maintain regular communication with your audience, bombarding inboxes can lead to subscriber fatigue. Analyze the behavior of your audience to determine the best times and frequencies for sending emails. Sometimes, less is more, especially if each email delivers value and maintains the anticipation for the next.

Lastly, it's essential to know that email marketing is a constantly evolving field. What worked yesterday may not work tomorrow, so stay curious and adaptable. Keep an eye on trends, experiment with new technologies, and always be willing to iterate on your strategies. The digital landscape is ever-changing, and staying ahead of the game is key to capturing and keeping your audience's attention.

In conclusion, when you've mastered the intricacies of social media, expanding your digital footprint through email marketing is not just the next step—it's a strategic leap. By following these guidelines and continually refining your approach based on data and feedback, you can turn your email list into a powerful asset that complements your social media empire. It's about building relationships, adding value, and engaging your audience in a way that goes beyond the transient nature of social feeds. Embrace the challenge, and watch your digital presence and influence grow like never before.

The Synergy Between Social Media and E-Commerce

In the digital era, the fusion between social media and e-commerce has created a dynamic platform for businesses and individual creators to not only grow their audiences but also to monetize their presence in unprecedented ways. This synergy has opened up a new realm of possibilities, empowering those ready to dive in with the right strategies.

The convergence of social media and e-commerce isn't just about pushing products or services through social channels; it's about creating a seamless experience that starts with content engagement and leads directly to sales opportunities without the user ever feeling bombarded by sales pitches. At its core, this relationship thrives on the authentic connections forged through engaging content and personalized interactions.

One fundamental aspect of leveraging this synergy lies in understanding the power of influence. Social media platforms have evolved into spaces where trust and authority are built through consistency, relatability, and providing value. These components, when harnessed correctly, can significantly impact purchasing decisions, making influencers and content creators incredibly valuable to e-commerce efforts.

Moreover, social media provides the perfect testing ground for products and marketing messages. Instant feedback mechanisms allow for real-time adjustments, making it easier to refine offerings and messaging to precisely match your audience's desires and needs. This feedback loop can drastically shorten the path to finding the most effective ways to present products or services, thereby increasing conversion rates.

The integration of shopping features on platforms like Instagram and Facebook has further blurred the lines between content and commerce. These features allow for direct purchases through the social media interface, creating a smooth transition from interest to acquisition. This direct integration not only simplifies the purchasing process but also keeps users engaged with the platform, fostering a more integrated user experience.

Another critical element is the use of user-generated content (UGC) in e-commerce strategies. UGC, such as reviews, unboxing videos, or product-related posts by users, has the power to influence potential customers more significantly than traditional advertising. By incorporating UGC into your social media strategy, you're not only showing real-life applications of your products but also building social proof that can drive sales.

Furthermore, leveraging social media for e-commerce goes beyond just selling products; it's about building a community around your brand. Engaging with your audience, responding to comments, and creating interactive content can foster a sense of belonging and loyalty. This community-building aspect is invaluable, as it turns casual shoppers into brand advocates who are more likely to make repeat purchases and recommend your brand to others.

Data-driven strategies also play a crucial role in maximizing the synergy between social media and e-commerce. By analyzing data from social media interactions, businesses can gain insights into consumer behavior and preferences, allowing for more targeted and effective marketing strategies. This data can inform everything from product development to personalized marketing campaigns, making your initiatives more relevant and appealing to your audience.

Another innovative approach is the use of live streaming to drive sales. Platforms like Instagram Live and Facebook Live offer unique opportunities to showcase products, conduct live demonstrations, or host Q&A sessions. These live interactions not only boost engagement but also create a sense of urgency and exclusivity, encouraging viewers to make immediate purchases.

It's also important to consider the role of mobile optimization in the fusion of social media and e-commerce. With the majority of social media engagement occurring on mobile devices, ensuring that your e-commerce processes are optimized for mobile is crucial. From the layout of your social media posts to the checkout process on your website, every aspect should be streamlined for mobile users to ensure a frictionless shopping experience.

Collaborations and partnerships can further enhance the e-commerce potential of your social media efforts. Partnering with other brands or influencers can introduce your products or services to new audiences, expanding your reach and potentially driving up sales. Such collaborations can also lend additional credibility to your offerings, tapping into the trust that these partners have already established with their followers.

Ambassador programs are another effective strategy, turning loyal customers into brand representatives on social media. These ambassadors can share their positive experiences with your products, offering authentic endorsements that resonate more profoundly with potential customers than traditional advertising.

Despite the vast opportunities, navigating the intersection of social media and e-commerce is not without challenges. Keeping content fresh and engaging while also driving sales requires a delicate balance. Furthermore, staying up to date with the constantly evolving features of social media platforms and consumer trends can be daunting. However, those who invest the time to understand and leverage these dynamics can reap significant rewards.

In conclusion, the synergy between social media and e-commerce represents a powerful tool for growth and monetization. By focusing on building authentic connections, leveraging platform features, and employing data-driven strategies, you can unlock the full potential of this dynamic duo. Remember, success in this space is not just about selling; it's about creating meaningful interactions and experiences that lead to lasting customer relationships and, ultimately, a thriving digital presence.

Embracing this synergy isn't just an option for those looking to expand their digital footprint; it's becoming a necessity. As we move forward, the integration of social media and e-commerce will only deepen, offering even more innovative ways to connect with and sell to your audience. The question is, are you ready to tap into this powerful combination and transform your approach to digital marketing and sales?

Conclusion

In concluding this journey, we've covered an extensive terrain of concepts, strategies, and actionable insights aimed at elevating your social media prowess. While the landscape of social media is perpetually morphing, the foundations we've laid together are designed to stand the test of time. It's essential to remember that at the heart of social media success lies the power of connection, creativity, and adaptability.

The evolution of social media from a casual communication channel to a significant marketplace has opened myriad opportunities. Harnessing these opportunities requires understanding that success on social media is not a fluke but a result of deliberate, calculated actions. From setting up your profiles for maximum impact to crafting content with viral potential, the importance of intentionality can't be overemphasized.

Mastering the algorithm, as we've seen, is both an art and a science. The algorithms are your invisible audience, constantly shifting, learning, and adapting. Staying ahead means being willing to pivot, to test new strategies, and to learn from the data. Engagement, the true currency of social media, hinges not on the number of followers but on the quality of interactions. Building genuine connections and fostering a sense of community will always outperform superficial metrics.

Monetization, a key goal for many, requires creativity beyond traditional advertising. It's about blending your unique voice and offerings with the needs and desires of your audience. It's a partnership with your followers, where value is exchanged in a multitude of ways, be it through partnerships, merchandise, or exclusive content.

Growth hacking, viral content, and engagement strategies are potent tools. Yet, they are merely components of a larger ecosystem. Understanding this ecosystem—its trends, its changes, and its constants—is crucial. The digital world's rapid evolution mandates a mindset geared towards continuous learning and flexibility.

As we've navigated through the intricacies of social media, from crafting impactful content to navigating the legal landscape, one theme has remained consistent: the importance of authenticity and ethical conduct. The trust of your audience is both a currency and a compass. It guides your strategies, shapes your content, and ultimately, fuels your growth.

Scaling your empire, an ambition many hold, relies on the solid foundation of a well-developed strategy, a deep understanding of your audience, and the efficient utilization of available tools and resources. Your social media journey is a reflection of your evolution, marked by milestones of innovation, engagement, and enduring connections.

As we look towards the future, the realms of artificial intelligence, global connectivity, and digital innovation promise to redefine what's possible. Staying informed, adaptable, and eager to explore new frontiers will empower you to not only navigate these changes but to thrive amidst them.

Ultimately, your success on social media is a testament to your commitment to your vision, your audience, and your message. In this digital age, where everyone has a voice, making yours resonate is both a challenge and an opportunity. May you approach this with the courage to be authentic, the ambition to innovate, and the wisdom to connect deeply.

Remember, in the dynamic world of social media, the only constant is change. As you move forward, take these lessons not as rigid directives but as guiding principles to adapt and apply in your unique journey. Here's to your success, in the ever-evolving landscape of social media!

Appendix A: Appendix

In your journey to cultivate a flourishing presence on social media, it's not just the strategies and concepts that matter, but also the tools and resources you have at your disposal. Having access to a comprehensive toolkit can significantly streamline your processes, enhance your content, deepen your analytical insights, and ultimately, empower your growth and monetization efforts. Here, we've compiled a selection of recommended tools and resources designed to support you across various dimensions of your social media endeavors.

Content Creation & Editing

- **Canva:** A user-friendly graphic design tool with thousands of templates to help create visually compelling social media posts, stories, and ads.

- **InShot:** Handy for editing videos directly on your phone, making it ideal for platforms that thrive on video content like Instagram, TikTok, and YouTube.

Analytics & Insights

- **Google Analytics:** Essential for tracking and analyzing traffic to your blog or website from your social media channels.

- **Social Blade:** Offers comprehensive analytics for YouTube, Twitter, Instagram, and Twitch, making it easier to track your growth and assess your performance.

Scheduling & Management

- **Buffer:** Great for scheduling posts, analyzing performance, and managing all your social media accounts from one dashboard.

- **Hootsuite:** Allows for bulk scheduling, real-time analytics, and monitoring multiple streams of content across your social platforms.

Growth & Engagement

- **BuzzSumo:** Identifies trending content and influencers across social media platforms, helping you to stay ahead of trends and engage with relevant topics.

- **Later:** Not just a scheduling tool, Later helps find the best times to post and provides insights on your audience's engagement.

Monetization & Collaboration

- **AspireIQ:** Connects you with brands for collaborations, helping to monetize your social media platforms through partnerships.

- **Shopify:** If you're considering selling merchandise or services, Shopify provides a comprehensive e-commerce platform to create your online store.

Legal & Ethical Considerations

While it's exciting to explore various tools and platforms for enhancing your social media presence, it's essential to navigate this digital landscape ethically and legally. Remember to respect copyright laws, protect the privacy of your community, and uphold transparency in your partnerships and sponsorships. Exploring the realms of creativity and innovation within these boundaries not only enhances your integrity but also builds trust with your audience.

Embracing these tools and resources can profoundly impact your efficiency, creativity, and the strategic depth of your social media campaigns. However, while this list serves as a foundation, always be on the lookout for emerging tools and technologies that can further amplify your reach and foster deeper connections with your audience. The landscape of social media is ever-evolving, and staying adaptable with the right tools at your disposal is key to mastering it.

Recommended Tools and Resources

We're diving into a toolkit that will not just amplify your social media game but also streamline the hefty process, making your journey to going viral, engaging with your audience, and monetization much smoother. Leverage these resources to tackle the social media algorithm head-on, ensuring your content isn't just seen but remembered and shared.

Content Creation & Editing Tools

Canva: Whether it's crafting eye-catching posts or designing ads that convert, Canva is your go-to design tool, especially if you're not a Photoshop expert. With a user-friendly interface and tons of templates, it makes design accessible to everyone.

InShot: When it comes to video editing on the go, InShot offers a comprehensive suite of tools that make it easy to edit videos right from your phone. From trimming clips to adding filters and music, it equips you with everything you need to create videos that captivate.

Analytics and Management

Google Analytics: Understanding your audience is vital, and Google Analytics provides deep insights into user behavior, helping you tailor your strategy to ensure it resonates with your target demographic.

Hootsuite: Managing multiple social media accounts can be daunting. Hootsuite simplifies it by allowing you to schedule posts, track the performance of your content, and manage all your social media profiles from a single dashboard.

Engagement Boosters

Quuu: Elevate your content strategy with hand-curated content recommendations that are relevant to your audience, boosting engagement through meaningful interactions.

Chatfuel: Integrate a chatbot on your Facebook page to instantly engage with followers, answer FAQs, or guide them through your content, enhancing the user experience and fostering a closer connection with your audience.

Monetization Platforms

Teachable: If you're looking to monetize your knowledge, Teachable is an exceptional platform to create and sell courses. Its intuitive course builder and marketing tools make it easy for you to turn your expertise into income.

Shopify: For social media influencers looking to sell merchandise or services, Shopify offers a seamless way to set up an online store that's fully integrated with your social media channels, simplifying the buying process for your audience.

Remember, while tools offer you a competitive edge, they're most effective when used as part of a well-thought-out strategy. Combine these resources with the insights and tactics shared throughout this book, and you'll be well on your way to building a formidable presence on social media. Experiment with what resonates best with your audience and don't shy away from pivoting your strategy based on analytics and engagement. Above all, stay true to your voice and vision, because authenticity is the cornerstone of any successful social media empire.

Glossary of Terms

In the vast and ever-evolving world of social media, a solid grasp of the terminology can be your anchor. Whether it's understanding the nuanced differences between 'engagement' and 'reach' or figuring out what exactly constitutes a 'meme', this glossary is designed to demystify the jargon. Here, you'll find definitions of key terms that will crop up throughout your journey to social media stardom.

Algorithm

An algorithm in the context of social media is a complex set of rules used by platforms to determine the visibility of content to users. This can include how posts are ranked in a feed, which content gets promoted, and personalization based on user behavior.

Analytics

Analytics refers to the collection and analysis of data related to your social media performance. Insights gleaned from analytics can tell you which of your posts are hitting the mark, how your audience is growing, and guide your content strategy.

Content Strategy

This is your game plan for what you're going to post on your social media platforms. It involves a detailed approach considering your objectives, target audience, and how you'll measure success. A robust content strategy balances quality and quantity while remaining adaptable.

Engagement

Engagement measures the extent to which your audience interacts with your content. This can include likes, comments, shares, and saves. High engagement rates are often seen as indicators of content that resonates well with an audience.

Hashtag

A hashtag is a word or phrase preceded by a hash mark (#) used within a social media post to identify a keyword or topic of interest and facilitate a search for it. Hashtags help increase the visibility of a post to those who might be interested in its subject matter.

Influencer

An influencer is an individual who has the power to affect the purchasing decisions of others because of their authority, knowledge, position, or relationship with their audience. Influencers typically have a sizable and engaged follower base on social media platforms.

Monetization

Monetization refers to the process of converting your social media activities into earnings. This can be achieved through various methods such as partnering with brands, selling merchandise, or utilizing ad revenue.

Niche

A niche is a specialized segment of the market for a particular kind of product or service. In social media, identifying your niche helps in crafting more focused, relevant content and building a targeted, engaged audience.

Reach

Reach is the total number of people who have seen your content. Unlike engagement, which measures interaction with your content, reach quantifies how far your content has traveled, including to those who aren't following you.

User-Generated Content (UGC)

User-Generated Content refers to any content—text, videos, images, reviews, etc.—created by people, rather than brands. On social media, encouraging UGC can enhance engagement, build community, and provide authentic material to share.

Understanding these terms is just the beginning. Each is a tool in your arsenal as you navigate your way through crafting a potent social media presence, grow your audience, and ultimately, achieve virality. Remember, the landscape is always changing; staying educated is your best strategy.

Further Reading

As we've journeyed together through the layers and dynamics of building a formidable presence on social media, it's clear that mastery is an ongoing process. The landscape of social media is ever-evolving, with new trends, algorithms, and platforms emerging regularly. To stay ahead, dipping into a well of diverse resources is crucial. Below, you'll find a curated list of reading materials that span across various facets of social media growth, engagement, and monetization. These suggestions are tailored to enhance your understanding and equip you with the insights needed to excel in the digital realm.

Books

- **Social Media Strategy:** A comprehensive guide delving into the strategic planning necessary for success across different social media platforms.

- **The Art of Social Media:** This eye-opening read provides tactical advice on creating content that resonates, building a loyal following, and leveraging social media for professional growth.

- **Contagious: How to Build Word of Mouth in the Digital Age:** A deep dive into what makes online content go viral and how you can craft messages that spread like wildfire.

Online Publications and Blogs

If books are the hearty meals of knowledge, think of online publications and blogs as the necessary snacks that keep you fueled with the latest trends, updates, and case studies. Here are a few to bookmark:

- *Social Media Examiner:* Renowned for its detailed articles and reports, this platform is a treasure trove of strategies and insights from social media experts.

- *Buffer Blog:* Apart from offering a popular social media management tool, Buffer shares actionable content marketing and strategy advice suitable for all levels of experience.

- *TechCrunch - Social:* For those interested in the intersection of technology and social media, TechCrunch offers updates on the latest tools, platforms, and tech trends shaping the digital landscape.

Podcasts

For those who prefer learning on the go, podcasts offer a dynamic way to absorb information. Here are a couple that should be on your playlist:

- **Social Media Marketing Podcast:** Dive into insightful interviews with leading social media professionals, unpacking strategies that yield real results.

- **The GaryVee Audio Experience:** While not exclusively about social media, Gary Vaynerchuk shares valuable lessons on marketing, entrepreneurship, and staying adaptable in the digital age.

In addition to these resources, don't underestimate the power of active participation in online forums and networking groups. Sharing experiences, asking questions, and staying engaged with a community of peers can provide practical insights and ongoing support as you navigate your social media journey.

Remember, the path to social media success is paved with continuous learning, experimentation, and adaptation. By incorporating these further reading suggestions into your growth plan, you're not just building a social media presence—you're cultivating a resilient, dynamic digital empire.

www.ingramcontent.com/pod-product-compliance
Lightning Source LLC
Chambersburg PA
CBHW051230050326
40689CB00007B/865